The Merrill Studies
in
The Sun Also Rises

Compiled by
William White
Wayne State University

Charles E. Merrill Publishing Company
A Bell & Howell Company
Columbus, Ohio

PS
3515
E37
S94

CHARLES E. MERRILL STUDIES

Under the General Editorship of
Matthew J. Bruccoli and Joseph Katz

Printed in the United States of America

Preface

With the publication of *The Sun Also Rises* in 1926, Ernest Hemingway (1899-1961) was established as an important American writer. He had already published two small books, *Three Stories & Ten Poems* (1923) and *in our time* (1924) by *avant garde* presses in Paris, which attracted little attention; *In Our Time* (1925), a revision of his second book and a considerable enlargement, issued in New York and distinguished from the earlier version by using initial capital letters in its title; *The Torrents of Spring* (1926), a piece of satirical fluff with a serious core; and *Today Is Friday* (1926) a play in a pamphlet. A few reviewers and critics recognized Hemingway's particular talent in the short stories of the New York *In Our Time:* thus they had prepared the serious reading public for his first generally accepted novel, *The Sun Also Rises*.

That the book was not immediately a great financial success does not really matter, though it did go through ten printings in three years and has since sold more than a million copies. As literature in the form of a novel, *The Sun Also Rises* was Hemingway's first success. It set forth, in full length, the Hemingway hero, the Hemingway code, the Hemingway style, and the Hemingway theme. These were to be repeated and enlarged upon, but not to any great extent, in everything he was to write from then on: four novels, *A Farewell to Arms* (1929), *To Have and Have Not* (1937), *For Whom the Bell Tolls* (1940), and *Across the River and Into the Trees* (1950); a novella, *The Old Man and the Sea* (1952); three collections of short stories, *Men Without Women* (1927),*Winner Take Nothing* (1933), *and The Fifth Column and the First Forty-nine Stories* (1938), which also includes a play; and three non-fiction books, *Death in the Afternoon* (1932), *Green Hills of Africa* (1935), and *A Moveable Feast* (1964), the last posthumous but largely prepared for publication by him.

Yet *The Sun Also Rises* has remained, in the eyes of many, the best and most important book by Ernest Hemingway. In evaluating his fiction, critics consider *The Old Man and the Sea*, fine work that it is and one which had much to do with his being awarded the Nobel Prize for Literature in 1954, a long short story and not meant to be a full-length work; *To Have and Have Not* and *Across and River and Into the Trees* are weak novels, which is about the kindest word one can say for the latter; and of the other two books, both *A Farewell to Arms* and *For Whom the Bell Tolls* have their champions as "the best of Hemingway," the Spanish civil war novel certainly considered the most ambitious work of the author.

My own preference is for *The Sun Also Rises*. Written first, when Hemingway was still in his twenties, it has all the spontaneity of youth — despite his traumatic experiences of World War I and post-war Paris — although it does not have smoothly polished artistic refinement of *The Old Man and the Sea*, which came with the years. The artistry and literary quality of *The Sun Also Rises* derived from, to use a phrase from a different context, blood, sweat, and tears; for no man worked harder at his craft than Hemingway, as a look at his manuscripts shows.

Not only is *The Sun Also Rises* the first and the best of its author's novels, it is, too, the most representative of his long writing: it has, as I have already indicated, what is generally regarded as typical Hemingway qualities in characters, setting, plot, and atmosphere — all put together in a way that is unmistakable in its uniqueness. A discussion of these world-weary, disillusioned men and women, in their alien cities and countrysides, going from place to place and indulging in their varied activities, and setting the peculiar tone of their imaginative and sometimes real world — all this is what the book reviewers, the scholars, and the critics do in the pieces I have selected for this anthology.

The first part of the collection is made up of periodical reviews, both from America and England, which were published when *The Sun Also Rises* appeared: Charles Scribner's Sons issued the book in New York on 22 October 1926; and Jonathan Cape issued it, as *Fiesta*, in London on 9 June 1927, omitting the quotations from Ecclesiastes (from which the American title, *The Sun Also Rises*, comes) and from Gertrude Stein ("You are all a lost generation").

The second part of the collection consists of longer, more detailed, and more fully considered discussions of the novel, sometimes in the context of Hemingway's career as a serious literary artist, one of the most important and stimulating in Twentieth Century American fiction.

WW

Contents

1. Contemporary Reviews

2. Essays

1. Contemporary Reviews

Conrad Aiken

Expatriates

It is rumored, with what accuracy I do not know, that Mr. Hemingway has at one time and another fought bulls in Spain as a mode of making a livelihood. Whether or not that is true, he writes of bull-fighting with extraordinary insight; he is clearly an expert. He is also, as clearly, *aficionado*—which is the Spanish term for a "fan." *Aficionado*, however, is a profounder word than fan, and suggests emotional intensities and religious zeals, not to mention psychotic fixations, which the baseball enthusiast does not dream of. If one likes bull-fighting, it has much the effect on one that half a course of psycho-analysis might have. One is thrilled and horrified; but one is also fascinated, and one cannot have enough. Perhaps the bull-fight only operates in this way on one who is too timid to descend into the ring himself—in which case one must absolve Mr. Hemingway from the charge of psychosis. Nevertheless, it is an interesting fact that his best short story, thus far, is a bull-fight story, "The Undefeated," which in tragic intensity and sparseness of outline challenges comparison with the very finest of contemporary short stories. And it is further interesting

From New York *Herald Tribune Books* (31 October 1926), 4.

that in his new novel, "The Sun Also Rises," the narrative works up to, and in a sense is built around, a bull-fight. Moreover, the story takes on, at this point, a force and tension which is nowhere else quite so striking.

This is not to suggest, however, that Mr. Hemingway's novel is lacking in these qualities, or that without the magnetism which the bull-fight exerts upon him he would be helpless. It has been apparent for some time that Mr. Hemingway is a writer of very unusual gifts; it has been merely a question as to what direction he would take. In "The Sun Also Rises" he takes a decided step forward and makes it possible for me to say of him, with entire conviction, that he is in many respects the most exciting of contemporary American writers of fiction. To say that his literary debts are obvious is not to mitigate this assertion in the slightest. He has learned something from Mr. Anderson, and something, perhaps, from Mr. Fitzgerald's "Great Gatsby": he may even have extracted a grain or two of ore from Miss Gertrude Stein—which is in itself no inconsiderable feat.

But in the accomplished fact his work is not in the least like the work of any of these writers. If one thing is striking about it, furthermore, it is the extraordinary individuality of style. His publishers say of him, with a discernment unusual in publishers, that he has contrived, in his novel, to present his people and his actions not as perceptible through a literary medium but as if immediate, and that is true. If once or twice in his story he slips into something of Mr. Anderson's cumbersome and roundabout explanatory method, with its "what I mean to say" and its "the thing is this," these echoes are few and unimportant. His own method lies at the other extreme. He simply states; he even, as a general rule, can be said to understate. It almost appears that he goes out of his way, now and then, to avoid the descriptive or the expansive methods—one has the feeling that he is a little afraid of being caught with any sort of purple on his palette, whether it be of rhetoric or of poetry. The action, he seems to say, must speak wholly for itself.

This results, as might be expected, in a quite extraordinary effect of honest and reality. The half dozen characters, all of whom belong to the curious and sad little world of disillusioned and aimless expatriates who make what home they can in the cafes of Paris, are seen perfectly and unsentimentally by Mr. Hemingway and are put before us with a maximum of economy. In the case of the hero, through whose mind we meet the event, and again in the cases of Brett, the heroine, and Robert Cohn, the sub-hero, Mr. Hemingway accomplishes more than this—he achieves an understanding and revelation of character which approaches the profound. When one reflects on the unattractiveness, not to say sordidness, of the scene, and the (on the whole) gracelessness of the people, one is all the more astonished at the fact that Mr. Hemingway should have made them so moving. These folk exist, that is all; and if their story is sordid, it is also, by virtue of the author's dignity and detachment in the telling, intensely tragic.

If one feature of "The Sun Also Rises" demands separate discussion, it is Mr. Hemingway's use of dialogue. The dialogue is brilliant. If there is better dialogue being written today I do not know where to find it. More than any other talk I can call to mind, it is alive with the rhythms and idioms, the pauses and suspensions and innuendoes and shorthands, of living speech. It is in the dialogue, almost entirely, that Mr. Hemingway tells his story and makes the people live and act. This is the dramatist's gift and it reminds one of those novels of Henry James which were first projected as plays and then written, with something like an excess of talk, as fiction. Will Mr. Hemingway try his hand at a play? He clearly has the ability to make his story move, and move with intensity, through the medium. It is possible that he overuses this ability. One occasionally longs for a slowing down and expansion of the medium, a pause for more leisurely luxuriation in the instant, such as Mr. Hemingway only vouchsafes us in the fishing episode and in the account of the *fiesta* and the bull-fight. James himself, despite his sins in this regard, somewhere remarked that dialogue, the most trenchant of the novelists' weapons, should be used as sparely as possible, to be kept in reserve, its force and edge unimpaired, for those scenes in which the action took a definite and decisive turn; it is above all in dialogue that climax should flower. In a sense, therefore, Mr. Hemingway gives us the feeling of finality and climax a little too often and thus deprives himself and his reader of that long curve of crescendo without which a novel lacks final perfection of form. His sparseness and economy, his objective detachment, would be only the more effective for an occasional offset, and his canvas greatly richer.

Ernest Boyd

Readers and Writers

Last June, when "The Torrents of Spring" was published, it was my pleasure to confess that the author, Ernest Hemingway, had enabled me to distinguish him from the surrounding Americans in Paris who contribute to esoteric Franco-American magazines, and now and then publish a volume in France which would not pass the vigilant scrutiny of American or English printers. The fact that one very great book, to wit, James Joyce's "Ulysses," was published in that manner had never converted me to the notion that any book printed in English in France must necessarily be the masterpiece of an expatriate and misunderstood genius. When Mr. Hemingway brought out his first volume of short stories, "In Our Time" (Liveright), I felt that anything he had to say might well be said over the imprint of an American publisher, and that he ought on no account to become the victim of that spurious fame attaching to books published in France and barred from this country.

With remarkable foresight Mr. Hemingway made the supreme sacrifice for an American of his generation; he left Paris for a few

From *The Independent*, CXVII (20 November 1926), 594.

weeks and rested his feet upon the barren soil of his native land. He rested them long enough to interest one of the oldest and most dignified publishing houses in America in two manuscripts, of which the second, "The Sun Also Rises" (Scribner's), has just appeared in direct and apostolic succession to "The Torrents of Spring." The latter, I may say, was regarded coldly by those who take their Sherwood Anderson straight, and it was even said that the author was that creature who is sharper than a serpent's tooth, namely, a thankless child. Mr. Hemingway, it seems, was an admirer, nay, a disciple, of Mr. Anderson, and in parodying him, he was biting the literary hand that had been outstretched to feed him at the outset of a great career. It was my impartial opinion that this base ingratitude was a hopeful sign of conversion.

"The Sun Also Rises" is a first offering from the convert, for which I return thanks unto the gods who thus touch the hearts of wayward men. The aura of æstheticism no longer lingers about Mr. Hemingway. Innocent of his past, one would never guess that he once toyed with synthetic heresies and bowed down to æsthetic idols of wood and stone. What one felt as a potential quality of certain stories in "In Our Time" is here realized with masterly cunning. It all looks so simple! He hasn't even a story to tell. There are no witty and no purple patches. Yet, when the book is finished, the reader has heard a story, his mind has been titillated by something which must obviously have been the author's sense of humor, and flashes of scenes remain in the memory despite his refusal to do more than hint at what he sees.

In the first place, Ernest Hemingway writes dialogue so effectively that he has merely to allow one to hear the sound of a character's voice in order to plant him vividly before the reader. Those familiar with the particular world of Paris which is the axis of the narrative will further note with amusement how Mr. Hemingway has managed to introduce several easily identified people, of minor importance intrinsically, but of deep importance as typical phenomena. Robert Cohn, who learned boxing "painfully and thoroughly to counteract the feeling of inferiority and shyness he had felt on being treated as a Jew at Princeton," is something more than an impression of a certain American editor in exile. His portrait becomes at Mr. Hemingway's hands an amazing character study.

Another figure who lives intensely in these pages, although her activities consist mainly of having drinks, lovers, and passionate moments of sincerity with the author's *alter ego*, is Lady Ashley, a perfect product of that postwar world of which Mr. Hemingway is the brilliant chronicler. After all that we have suffered from novelists intent on describing hardboiled flappers, Ernest Hemingway comes along with his modern version of *la femme de trente ans*, and we know more about the eternal feminine, model 1926, than ever before. If there are people who wonder why six cocktails grow where one grew before, this book will tell them. The consumption of liquor to the square inch in "The Sun Also Rises" reaches maximum pressure, and just as these characters would not exist without their frequent and generous libations, so, I think, Mr. Hemingway's story could not be told within the limits of what is so preposterously known in this country as "Law Enforcement" — meaning usually the illegal imposition of one measure.

Mr. Hemingway is not merely a student of expatriate alcoholism, he is a bullfighting connoisseur, and when his group of tragic comedians arrive in Pamplona for the *fiesta*, he dwells with an expert's affection upon every aspect of the affair without once giving the impression that he is determined to show how much he knows. He enters into the technicalities and leaves the picturesque to emerge as best it can, and it does emerge more truly and impressively than from any bravura passage. The reason being that the technical details of a bullfight are no more and no less to the author than the details of the innumerable drinks and dishes consumed in the course of that hectic week. All these matters are equal in the sight of Mr. Hemingway, and with the utmost gravity, certain in managing his effects, he carefully records exactly what each person drinks or does.

The technique of this book is fascinating. When one is not swept along by astonishing dialogue, subtle, obvious, profound, and commonplace, — but always alive, — one is listening to careful enumeration of little facts whose cumulative effect is to give them the importance of remarkable incidents. The description of Pamplona during the festival week is reporting of the most laconic type. We are told what preparations are made, we see the bulls being unloaded from the train, the peasants swarming in from the countryside, and we are plunged into tavern brawls and carouses. At no time does the author attempt to "write up" his scenes, but in the end one has the feeling of having spent the week there.

In the midst of all this Mr. Hemingway never loses sight of his psychological *déracinés*, who so strongly merge their highly complicated modern selves in the stream of elementary consciousness. Remote as they seem from the setting, they are a part of it. Fishing in Spain or drinking at Zelli's, these American men express themselves, the curious syncopated rhythm of their lives, just as Frances, the American girl, endures in a nagging scene outside a café, and Brett, the Englishwoman, bares her soul in fierce moments of tortured feeling. Ernest Hemingway has so completely realized his types and mastered his medium that he triumphantly adds a new chapter to the story which Scott Fitzgerald began in "This Side of Paradise."

Cleveland B. Chase

Out of Little, Much

The sense of unbounded vigor and enthusiasm coolly repressed and controlled that characterized Ernest Hemingway's book of short stories, "In Our Time," is also the most striking feature of this notable first novel. Written in terse, precise, and aggressively fresh prose, and containing some of the finest dialogue yet written in this country, the story achieves a vividness and a sustained tension that make it unquestionably one of the events of a year rich in interesting books.

Nothing, the adjective is used advisedly, that Hemingway describes has ever been more convincingly described. It probably never will be; for while he writes with spareness and economy, his gift for seizing upon the essential qualities of whatever occupies his attention leaves the reader with nothing to learn. There is a truly Shakespearian absoluteness about his writing. But the things he writes about—bull fights, Spanish fiestas, shallow philanderings, and the petty subtleties of café disputes and *amours* — seem scarcely worthy of the care, of the artistic integrity which he devotes to them.

From *The Saturday Review of Literature,* III (11 December 1926), 420-421. Reprinted by permission of the *Saturday Review.*

It would have been difficult for Mr. Hemingway to have chosen a more dreary or aimless setting for a novel. Having picked, apparently at random, a handful of those disillusioned and degenerating expatriates who make their headquarters in the cafés along the Boulevard Montparnasse, in Paris, he sends them on a fishing expedition to the Pyrennees which ends up in a week of riotous drunkenness at a fiesta and bull fight at Pamplona. He describes these people with photographic exactness. Anyone who is acquainted with the habitués of the cafés of the Boulevard Montparnasse will recognize most of the characters at once. Not one of them, I think, is the product of the author's imagination. Even the fishing trip about which the story centers is an actual event that took place, if my memory is not at fault, in the spring of 1924.

If the characters are intrinsically uninteresting, it is the greater tribute to the power of the author's style that the story never loses an almost painful tension. It is a supreme triumph of style over matter, and if the reader be tempted to question whether the triumph is real, let him turn to almost any one of Mr. Hemingway's passages of dialogue. As, for instance:

"Sit down," said Harvey, "I've been looking for you."

"What's the matter?"

"Nothing. Just looking for you."

"Been out to the races?"

"No. Not since Sunday."

"What do you hear from the States?"

"Nothing. Absolutely nothing."

"What's the matter?"

"I don't know. I'm through with them. I'm absolutely through with them."

He leaned forward and looked me in the eye.

"Do you want to know something, Jake?"

"Yes."

"I haven't had anything to eat for five days."

I figured rapidly back in my mind. It was three days ago that Harvey had won two hundred francs from me shaking poker dice in the New York bar.

"What's the matter?"

"No money. Money hasn't come," he paused. "I tell you it's strange, Jake. When I'm like this I just want to be alone. I want to stay in my own room. I'm like a cat."

I felt in my pocket.

"Would a hundred help you any, Harvey?"

"Yes."

"Come on. Let's go and eat."
"There's no hurry. Have a drink."
"Better eat."
"No. When I get like this I don't care whether I eat or not."
We had a drink. Harvey added my saucer to his own pile.

Mr. Hemingway's most pronounced gift as a writer is his ability
to seize upon the precise details in any setting or situation that
lend it meaning and individuality. In consequence he has developed
a crisp, terse, staccato style which consists largely in setting down
innumerable details, which are left to be fused and blended in the
reader's mind. . . .

And so in short, abrupt sentences he piles up details—petty,
unimportant details, details that are frequently on the verge of
being boring. "In the morning I walked down the boulevard to
the rue Soufflot for coffee and brioche. It was a fine morning. The
horse-chestnut trees in the Luxembourg gardens were in bloom. I
read the papers with the coffee and then smoked a cigarette. . . ."
"Why," we are tempted to exclaim, "not leave something to our
imagination?" But in the end he justifies his method. By the very
profuseness and precision of his details he achieves an eventual
economy that is astounding. There is a cumulative richness in his
staccato statements of fact. He says one thing, implies another,
while the whole atmosphere of a passage implies infinitely more
than is to be found in its individual parts. We find ourselves in the
presence of unsuspected subtleties of mood and of emotion which
are arrived at not through the medium of an author's hyperbolic
and roundabout statement of them, but because their essential
qualities are actually present upon the printed page. It is an
interesting fact that neither in his short stories nor in this novel
does Hemingway make use of a single simile. To him things are
not "like" other things. He does not write about them until he has
been able to grasp their essential qualities.

In his choice of these details Hemingway shows an amazing
penetration. Perhaps it is the tilt of a girl's head, or the harsh
light of an acetylene flare, or the attitude of a man giving a tip.
Whatever it is he sees it and without interpretation he sets it down,
relying for his effect upon the perfect relation and balance of the
details. Where Dreiser, for instance, has to spend pages upon a
minute record of everything about a situation, for fear the essential
quality of it will escape him, Hemingway writes with an economy
and precision engendered by his supreme self-confidence and his
unfailing knowledge of what is "right."

Lawrence S. Morris

Warfare in Man and among Men

To anyone with an eye on what was coming, Ernest Hemingway's short stories in the volume, In Our Time, were the most stirring pages of imaginative prose by an American which appeared last year. This man was molding an idiom of his own to express his own way of feeling and seeing. Now comes his first novel, The Sun Also Rises, and it is clear that the shorter tales were merely a preparation. No one need be afraid any more that Hemingway's power is going to be limited to episodes. He has shown that he can not only state a theme, but develop it.

His approach to his job is so direct that it appears casual. Any café or hotel room will do him for a setting. He drops his characters in and lets them live. He does not explain them, as a less complete artist would. He does not label their motives with generalizations of love, hate, ambition. He watches their behavior. Seen from without, his people act in hard, direct ways; from within it is plain there is no direction whatever. They are stumbling through life like a man lost in a forest: attracted to this side by what appears to be a clearing, repelled when the clearing is found to be a marsh.

From *The New Republic*, LXIX (22 December 1926), 142-143. Reprinted by permission of *The New Republic*.

The essential characteristic of our time is that it is a period without a generalization. Without a mythology, if you prefer: we have inherited a hundred mythologies, and our minds flutter among them, finding satisfaction in none. The distress we are all acutely aware of comes from our failure to realize this fact emotionally. Intellectually we have cut down these frameworks into which our predecessors fitted experience. But we have received new information too fast to digest it. We have not yet reached the full realization that these familiar frameworks are gone from our minds; in practice we cling to their shadows and are hurt when they fail to support us. Until we are emotionally convinced that the old values are gone, we shall not begin to lay down our own generalizations. We have reached the stage—familiar in the history of cultures—where we must pass through Ecclesiastes before writing our Revelations. All contemporary art that is vital, that has its roots in our immediate problem, must seem destructive. It is concerned in realizing this desperate purposeless by objectifying it.

The Sun Also Rises is one stride toward that objectification. The clear boundaries which were formerly assumed to define motives are gone. Very well: Hemingway will not try to make use of them, and will admit in his vocabulary only words which he himself has found solid. By this courageous self-denial—the mark of every genuine originality—he has achieved a style as close to his thought as the bone of which the skeleton is made is close to the skeleton; and firm with the firmness of packed sand and running water. The effect of this accuracy is a great gain in intensity. Between the lines of the hard-boiled narrative quivers an awareness of the unworded, half-grasped incomprehensibles of life.

The reader finds the characters of The Sun Also Rises gathered in Paris: an American newspaper correspondent; a Greek Count, with business experience in the Middle West; Cohn, who had graduated from Princeton and written a book; an English bankrupt; and Brett, who was the pivot of the group. Brett was a young Englishwoman, who was getting a divorce from a man she had never loved, to marry another whom she did not love, either. The development of their relations is seen through the eyes of the newspaper correspondent, who had been rendered impotent by a wound received in the War—a brutally efficient symbol of "a lost generation." It was he whom Brett loved and who loved Brett. From Paris the group migrates to the Pyrenees and shares in a week's fiesta in a Spanish town. The peak of the fiesta is the bull fights; and Hemingway gives her the only account in English of a bull fight known to this reviewer, in which the emphasis is laid not on cruelty, but on the steely beauty of skill, the perfection of workmanship in the face of danger. A bull fight becomes a hard, beautiful dance, where an awkwardness means death. Amid the rioting of the fiesta and the clear, breath-taking scenes in the bull ring, the group of characters plays its little tragedy of futility.

Although Hemingway is objectifying the bewildered anguish of an aimless generation, he does not moon about it. His mind is masculine and imaginative. He loves all the hard, stinging experiences of the senses, he loves skill, he can laugh. He knows the intonations and obliquenesses of human speech. No other American, writing today, can match his dialogue for its apparent naturalness, its intimacy and its concealed power of revealing emotion. Ring Lardner's in comparison sounds framed and self-conscious. For something against which to measure the use of overtones in Hemingway's talk one must go to Joyce's account of a Christmas dinner in the Portrait of an Artist or—allowing for the greater intellectual scope and intensity of Joyce's mind—to the quarrel between Leopold Bloom and the Citizen in Ulysses.

Edwin Muir

Fiction [*Fiesta*, by Ernest Hemingway]

Mr. Hemingway is a writer of quite Unusual talent. His observation is so exact that it has the effect of imagination; it evokes scenes, conversations, characters. His dialogue is by turns extraordinarily natural and brilliant, and impossibly melodramatic; when he has to describe anything he has a sureness and economy which recall Maupassant; he neither turns away from unpleasant details, nor does he stress them. There is, however, a curious inequality among his characters. Brett, the heroine, might have stepped out of "The Green Hat"; she is the sentimentally regarded dare-devil, and she never becomes real. But most of the other characters, the majority of them American Bohemians living in Paris, are graphically drawn. The original merits of the book are striking; its fault, equally apparent after one's first pleasure, is a lack of artistic significance. We see the lives of a group of people laid bare, and we feel that it does not matter to us. Mr. Hemingway tells us a great deal about those people, but he tells us nothing of importance about human life. He tells us nothing, indeed, which

Reprinted from *The Nation and Athenaeum* by permission of the New Statesman (London), XLI (2 July 1927), 450, 452.

15

any of his characters might not tell us; he writes with honesty, but as a member of the group he describes; and, accordingly, his narrative lacks proportion, which is the same thing as significance. But he is still a young writer; his gifts are original; and this first novel raises hopes of remarkable achievement. The Spanish scenes, Cohen's fight with the matador, the dance in the streets, the bull fight—these bring us in contact with a strong and original visual world.

Allen Tate

Hard-Boiled

The present novel by the author of "In Our Time" supports the recent prophecy that he will be the "big man in American letters." At the time the prophecy was delivered it was meaningless because it was equivocal. Many of the possible interpretations now being eliminated, we fear it has turned out to mean something which we shall all regret. Mr. Hemingway has written a book that will be talked about, praised, perhaps imitated; it has already been received in something of that cautiously critical spirit which the followers of Henry James so notoriously maintain toward the master. Mr. Hemingway has produced a successful novel, but not without returning some violence upon the integrity achieved in his first book. He decided for reasons of his own to write a popular novel, or he wrote the only novel which he could write.

To choose the latter conjecture is to clear his intentions, obviously at the cost of impugning his art. One infers moreover that although sentimentality appears explicitly for the first time in his prose, it must have always been there. Its history can be constructed. The method used in "In Our Time" was *pointilliste*, and

From *The Nation*, CXXIII (15 December 1926), 642, 644. Reprinted by permission of *The Nation*.

the sentimentality was submerged. With great skill he reversed the usual and most general formula of prose fiction: instead of selecting the details of physical background and of human behavior for the intensification of a dramatic situation, he employed the minimum of drama for the greatest possible intensification of the observed object. The reference of emphasis for the observed object was therefore not the action; rather, the reference of the action was the object, and the action could be impure or incomplete without risk of detection. It could be mixed and incoherent; it could be brought in when it was advantageous to observation, or left out. The exception, important as such, in Mr. Hemingway's work is the story Mr. and Mrs. Elliott. Here the definite dramatic conflict inherent in a sexual relation emerged as fantasy, and significantly; presumably he could not handle it otherwise without giving himself away.

In "The Sun Also Rises," a full-length novel, Mr. Hemingway could not escape such leading situations, and he had besides to approach them with a kind of seriousness. He fails. It is not that Mr. Hemingway is, in the term which he uses in fine contempt for the big word, hard-boiled; it is that he is not hard-boiled enough, in the artistic sense. No one can dispute with a writer the significance he dervies from his subject-matter; one can only point out that the significance is mixed or incomplete. Brett is a nymphomaniac; Robert Cohn, a most offensive cad; both are puppets. For the emphasis is false; Hemingway doesn't fill out his characters and let them stand for themselves; he isolates one or two chief traits which reduce them to caricature. His perception of the physical object is direct and accurate; his vision of character, singularly oblique. And he actually betrays the interior machinery of his hard-boiled attitude: "It is awfully easy to be hard-boiled about everything in the daytime, but at night it is another thing," says Jake, the sexually impotent, musing on the futile accessibility of Brett. The history of his sentimentality is thus complete.

There are certain devices exploited in the book which do not improve it; they extend its appeal. Robert Cohn is not only a bounder, he is a Jewish bounder. The other bounders, like Mike, Mr. Hemingway for some reason spares. He also spares Brett— another device—for while her pleasant folly need not be flogged, it equally need not be condoned; she becomes the attractive wayward lady of Sir Arthur Pinero and Michael Arlen. Petronius's Circe, the archetype of all the Bretts, was neither appealing nor deformed.

Mr. Hemingway has for some time been in the habit of throwing pebbles at the great—which recalls Mr. Pope's couplet about his contemporary Mr. Dennis. The habit was formed in "The Torrents of Spring," where it was amusing. It is disconcerting in the present novel; it strains the context; and one suspects that Mr. Hemingway protests too much. The point he seems to be making is that he is morally superior, for instance, to Mr. Mencken, but it is not yet clear just why.

Sad Young Man

A lot of people expected a big novel from burly young Author Hemingway. His short work (*In Our Time*, 1925) bit deeply into life. He said things naturally, calmly, tersely, accurately. He wrote only about things he had experienced mostly outdoors, as a doctor's son in northern Michigan and as a self-possessed young tramp in Europe. Philosophically his implication was: "Life's great. Don't let it rattle you."

Now his first novel is published and while his writing has acquired only a few affectations, his interests appear to have grown soggy with much sitting around sloppy café tables in the so-called Latin (it should be called American) quarter of Paris. He has chosen to immortalize the semi-humorous love tragedy of an insatiable young English War widow and an unmanned U. S. soldier. His title is borrowed from *Ecclesiastes;* his motto about "a lost generation," from Gertrude Stein; his widow Lady Brett Ashley, from Michael Arlen's *Green Hat*. She is repeatedly called "a nice piece," and "a good chap." She has a grim wit and not a shred of reticence. The hero failing, her other men are many, in-

From *Time,* VIII (1 November 1926), 48. Copyright © Time Inc. 1926. Reprinted by permission of Time, Inc.

cluding a Princeton Jew and a Spanish bullfighter. The story, such as it is, comes from the eunuch, Jake, who is very generous, patient, clever and, of course, very sad.

The picture of cosmopolitan castaways going to prizefights, bars, bedrooms, bullrings in France and Spain is excessively accurate but not as trite as it might be. The ironic witticisms are amusing, for a few chapters. There is considerable emotion, consciously restrained, quite subtle. Experts may pronounce the book a masterpiece of sex-frustration psychology. But the reader is very much inclined to echo a remark that is one of Jake's favorites and, presumably, Author Hemingway's too, "Oh, what the hell!"

Fiesta

In his first volume of short stories Mr. Ernest Hemingway got some very delicate and unusual effects by retranslating his impressions, as it were, into a primitive kind of imagery. He described his characters and their behaviour with deliberate naivety, identifying what they did and what they felt in an artful and extremely suggestive manner. Now comes a novel, FIESTA (Cape, 7s. 6d. net), which is more obviously an experiment in story-making, and in which he abandons his vivid impressionism for something much less interesting. There are moments of sudden illumination in the story, and throughout it displays a determined reticence; but it is frankly tedious after one has read the first hundred pages and ceased to hope for anything different. This is criticism we should not think of applying to the work of a less talented writer. The crude, meaningless conversation which Mr. Hemingway gives us is best taken for granted; it may be true to life, as the saying is, but there is hardly any point in putting it into a novel. Besides, so much of its consists of offers of drink and the bald confession of drunkenness that what virtue it has is staled by repetition.

Reproduced from *The Times Literary Supplement* (London, 30 June 1927), 454, by permission.

Drink, indeed, is an extraordinary bugbear for these Americans in Paris, almost more troublesome than sex. However, they are all artists, and it seems to be the artistic lot to be able to consume quantities of liquid which would send most human beings to the grave. Brett, the heroine, is scarcely ever sober; Jake, who loves her, but who has been smashed up in the war (it is terrible irony that Mr. Hemingway intends—and partly achieves— here), is a reserved, rather sardonic creature, and almost the only credible person in the story. His position lends some persuasiveness to Brett's nymphomania, although it does not make her less tiresome. The other men who love her or live with her are unexciting; Cohn is a caricature, Mike never comes to life, the young matador is a mixture of perversity and convention. The Spanish scenes give us something of the quality of Mr. Hemingway's earlier book, but they hardly qualify the general impression of an unsuccessful experiment.

2. Essays

Carlos Baker

The Way It Was

"The job of the last twenty-five years was for the writer or artist to get what there was to be got (artistically) out of the world extant."

—*Ezra Pound*[1]

"A writer's job is to tell the truth," said Hemingway in 1942.[2] He had believed it for twenty years and he would continue to believe it as long as he lived. No other writer of our time has so fiercely asserted, so pugnaciously defended, or so consistently exemplified the writer's obligation to speak truly. His standard of truth-telling has been, moreover, so high and so rigorous that he has very rarely been willing to admit secondary evidence, whether literary evidence or evidence picked up from other sources than his own experience. "I only know what I have seen," is a statement which comes often to his lips and pen. What he has personally done, or what he knows unforgettably by having gone through one version of it, is what he is interested in telling about. This is

From *Hemingway: The Writer as Artist* (Princeton, N. J.: Princeton University Press, 1956), 48-59. Copyright 1956 by the Princeton University Press. Reprinted by permission of Princeton University Press.
[1]Ezra Pound, quoted in Samuel Putnam, *Paris Was Our Mistress* (New York 1947), p. 154.
[2] *Men at War* (New York, 1942), introduction, p. xv.

not to say that he has refused to invent freely. But he has always made it a sacrosanct point to invert in terms of what he actually knows from having been there.

The primary intent of his writing, from first to last, has been to seize and project for the reader what he has often called "the way it was." This is a characteristically simple phrase for a concept of extraordinary complexity, and Hemingway's conception of its meaning has subtly changed several times in the course of his career—always in the direction of greater complexity. At the core of the concept, however, one can invariably discern the operation of three esthetic instruments: the sense of place, the sense of fact, and the sense of scene.

The first of these, which is clearly a passion with Hemingway, is the sense of place. "Unless you have geography, background," he once told George Antheil, "you have nothing."[3] You have, that is to say, a dramatic vacuum. Few writers have been more place-conscious. Few have so carefully charted out the geographical groundwork of their novels while managing to keep background so conspicuously unobtrusive. Few, accordingly, have been able to record more economically and graphically the way it is when you walk through the streets of Paris in search of breakfast at a corner café. Or when your footfalls echo among surrounding walls on the ancient cobblestones of early morning Venice, heading for the market-place beside the Adriatic. Or when, at around six o'clock of a Spanish dawn, you watch the bulls running from the corrals at the Puerta Rochapea through the streets of Pamplona towards the bullring.

"When I woke it was the sound of the rocket exploding that announced the release of the bulls from the corrals at the edge of town. . . . Down below the narrow street was empty. All the balconies were crowded with people. Suddenly a crowd came down the street. They were all running, packed close together. They passed along and up the street toward the bullring and behind them came more men running faster, and then some stragglers who were really running. Behind them was a little bare space, and then the bulls, galloping, tossing their heads up and down. It all went out of sight around the corner. One man fell, rolled to the gutter, and lay quiet. But the bulls went right on and did not notice him. They were all running together."[4]

[3] George Antheil, *Bad Boy of Music*, p. 278.
[4] *SAR*, pp. 165-166.

This scene is as morning-fresh as a design in India ink on clean white paper. First is the bare white street, seen from above, quiet and empty. Then one sees the first packed clot of runners. Behind these are the thinner ranks of those who move faster because closer to the bulls. Then the almost comic stragglers, who are "really running." Brilliantly behind these shines the "little bare space," a desperate margin for error. Then the clot of running bulls— closing the design, except of course for the man in the gutter making himself, like the designer's initials, as inconspicuous as possible.

The continuing freshness of such occasions as this might be associated with Hemingway's lifelong habit of early waking. More likely, the freshness arises because Hemingway loves continental cities, makes it almost a fetish to know them with an artist's eye, and has trained himself rigorously to see and retain those aspects of a place that make it *that place*, even though, with an odd skill, he manages at the same time to render these aspects generically.

As with the cities—and Hemingway's preference is for the Latin cities—so with the marshes, rivers, lakes, troutstreams, gulfstreams, groves, forests, hills, and gullies, from Wyoming to Tanganyika, from the Tagliamento to the Irati, and from Key West to the Golden Horn. "None can care for literature itself," said Stevenson, somewhere, "who do not take a special pleasure in the sound of names." Hemingway's love of names is obvious. It belongs to his sense of place. But like the rest of his language, it is under strict control. One never finds, as so often happens in the novels of Thomas Wolfe or the poetry of Carl Sandburg, the mere riot and revel of place-names, played upon like guitar-strings for the music they contain. Hemingway likes the words *country* and *land*. It is astonishing how often they recur in his work without being obtrusive. He likes to move from place to place, and to be firmly grounded, for the time being, in whatever place he has chosen. It may be the banks of the Big Two-Hearted River of Northern Michigan or its Spanish equivalent above Burguete. It may be the Guadarrama hilltop where El Sordo died, or the Veneto marshes where Colonel Cantwell shot his last mallards from a duckblind. Wherever it is, it is solid and permanent, both in itself and in the books.

The earliest of his published work, descriptively speaking, shows an almost neoclassical restraint. Take a sample passage from *The Sun Also Rises*, not his earliest but fairly representative. This one concerns the Irati Valley fishing-trip of Jake Barnes and Bill Gorton.

"It was a beech wood and the trees were very old. Their roots bulked above the ground and the branches were twisted. We walked on the road between the thick trunks of the old beeches and the sunlight came through the leaves in light patches on the grass. The trees were big, and the foilage was thick but it was not gloomy. There was no undergrowth, only the smooth grass, very green and fresh, and the big gray trees were well spaced as though it were a park. 'This is country,' Bill said."[5]

It is such country as an impressionist might paint almost exactly in the terms, and the subdued colors, which Hemingway employs. More than this, however, is the fact that in such a paragraph Dr. Samuel Johnson's Imlac could find little to criticize. Even the arrangement of the beech trees themselves, like the choice of the words, is clean and classical. The foliage is thick, but there is no gloom. Here is neither teeming undergrowth nor its verbal equivalent. The sage of Johnson's *Rasselas* advises all aspirant poets against numbering the streaks of the tulip or describing in detail the different shades of the verdure of the forest. Young Hemingway, still an aspirant poet, follows the advice. When he has finished, it is possible to say (and we supply our own inflection for Bill Gorton's words): "This is country."

For all the restraint, the avoidance of color flaunting adjectives, and the plainsong sentences (five compound to one complex), the paragraph is loaded with precisely observed fact: beech wood, old trees, exposed roots, twisted branches, thick trunks, sun-patches, smooth green grass, foliage which casts a shade without excluding light. One cannot say that he has been given a generalized landscape—there are too many exact factual observations. On the other hand, the uniquenesses of the place receive no special emphasis. One recognizes easily the generic type of the clean and orderly grove, where weeds and brush do not flourish because of the shade, and the grass gets only enough light to rise to carpet-level. Undoubtedly, as in the neoclassical esthetic, the intent is to provide a generic frame within which the reader is at liberty to insert his own uniquenesses—as many or as few as his imagination may supply.

Along with the sense of place, and as a part of it, is the sense of fact. Facts march through all his pages in a stream as continuous as the refugee wagons in Thrace or the military camions on the road from the Isonzo. Speculation, whether by the author or by

---

[5] *SAR,* p. 120.

the characters, is ordinarily kept to a minimum. But facts, visible or audible or tangible facts, facts baldly stated, facts without verbal paraphernalia to inhibit their striking power, are the stuff of Hemingway's prose.

Sometimes, especially in the early work, the facts seem too many for the effect apparently intended, though even here the reader should be on guard against misconstruing the intention of a given passage. It is hard to discover, nevertheless, what purpose beyond the establishment of the sense of place is served by Barnes's complete itinerary of his walk with Bill Gorton through the streets of Paris.[6] The direction is from Madame Lecomte's restaurant on the Ile St. Louis across to the left bank of the Seine, and eventually up the Boulevard du Port Royal to the Café Select. The walk fills only two pages. Yet it seems much longer and does not further the action appreciably except to provide Jake and Bill with healthy after-dinner exercise. At Madame Lecomte's (the facts again), they have eaten "a roast chicken, new green beans, mashed potatoes, a salad, and some apple pie and cheese." To the native Parisian, or a foreigner who knows the city, the pleasure in the after-dinner itinerary would consist in the happy shock of recognition. For others, the inclusion of so many of the facts of municipal or gastronomic geography—so many more than are justified by their dramatic purpose—may seem excessive.

Still, this is the way it was that time in Paris. Here lay the bridges and the streets, the squares and the cafés. If you followed them in the prescirbed order, you came to the café where Lady Brett Ashley sat on a high stool at the bar, her crossed legs stockingless, her eyes crinkling at the corners.

If an imaginative fusion of the sense of place and the sense of fact is to occur, and if, out of the fusing process, dramatic life is to arise, a third element is required. This may be called the sense of scene. Places are less than geography, facts lie inert and uncoordinated, unless the imagination runs through them like a vitalizing current and the total picture moves and quickens. How was it, for example, that second day of the San Fermin fiesta in the Pamplona bullring after Romero had killed the first bull?

"They had hitched the mules to the dead bull and then the whips cracked, the men ran, and the mules, straining forward, their legs pushing, broke into a gallop, and the bull, one horn up, his head on its side, swept a swath smoothly across the sand and out the red gate."[7]

---

[6] *SAR*, pp. 79-80.
[7] *SAR*, p. 175.

Here are a dead bull, men, mules, whips, sand, and a red gate like a closing curtain—the place and the facts. But here also, in this remarkably graphic sentence, are the seven verbs, the two adverbs, and the five adverbial phrases which fuse and coordinate the diverse facts of place and thing and set them in rapid motion. If one feels that the sentence is very satisfying as a scene, and wishes to know why, the answer might well lie where it so often lies in a successful lyric poem—that is, in our sense of difficulty overcome. Between the inertness of the dead bull when he is merely *hitched* (a placid verb) and the smooth speed with which the body finally *sweeps* across the sand and out of sight, come the verbs of sweating effort: *crack, run, strain,* and *break.* It is precisely at the verb *broke,* that the sentence stops straining and moves into the smooth glide of its close. The massing, in that section of the sentence, of a half-dozen s's, compounded with the *th* sounds of *swath* and *smoothly,* can hardly have been inadvertent. They ease (or grease) the path of the bull's departure.

The pattern in the quoted passage is that of a task undertaken, striven through, and smoothly completed: order and success. For another graphic sentence, so arranged as to show the precise opposites—total disorder and total failure—one might take the following example from *Death in the Afternoon.* The protagonist is a "phenomenon," a bullfighter who has lost his nerve.

"In your mind you see the phenomenon, sweating, white faced, and sick with fear, uable to look at the horn or go near it, a couple of swords on the ground, capes all around him, running in at an angle on the bull hoping the sword will strike a vital spot, cushions sailing down into the ring and the steers ready to come in."[8]

In this passage, place has become predicament. The facts, thrown in almost helter-skelter, imply the desperate inward fear which is responsible for the creation of the outward disorder. Verbs are held to a minimum, and their natural naked power is limited with qualifications. The phenomenon is *unable to look,* and *hoping to strike,* not *looking* and *striking.* He runs, but it is at a bad angle. The disorder of the swords on the ground and the capes all around is increased by the scaling-in of seat-cushions from the benches, the audience's insult to gross cowardice. The author-spectator's crowning insult is the allusion to the steers, who by comparison with the enraged bull are bovine, old-womanly creatures. On being admitted to the ring, they will quiet and lead away the bull the phenomenon could not kill.

---

[8] *DIA,* p. 226.

The sense of place and the sense of fact are indispensable to Hemingway's art. But the true craft, by which diversities are unified and compelled into graphic collaboration, comes about through the operation of the sense of scene. Often, moving through the Latin language countries, watching the crowd from a café table or a barrera bench, Hemingway seems like a lineal descendant of Browning's observer in *How It Strikes a Contemporary*.

> You saw go up and down Valladolid
> A man of mark, to know next time you saw . . .
> Scenting the world, looking it full in face.

Although they are clearly fundamental to any consideration of Hemingway's esthetic aims, place, fact, and scene are together no more than one phase of a more complex observational interest. The skillful writer can make them work in harmony, with place and fact like teamed horses under the dominance of the sense of scene. The result is often as striking and satisfactory to watch as a good chariot race. But the event is, after all, mainly an extrinsic matter. These are not Plato's horses of the soul.

The complementary phase is inward: a state of mind causally related to the extrinsic events and accurately presented in direct relation to those events. When Samuel Putnam asked Hemingway in the late twenties for a definition of his aims, the answer was: "Put down what I see and what I feel in the best and simplest way I can tell it."[9] Taken as absolute standards, of course, bestness and simplicity will often be at variance, a fact of which Hemingway at that date was apparently becoming more and more conscious. But his aim from the beginning had been to show, if he could, the precise relationship between what he saw and what he felt.

It is characteristic of Hemingway, with his genuine scorn for overintellectualized criticism, that he has himself refused to employ critical jargon in the presentation of his esthetic ideas. It is also evident, however, that early in his career, probably about 1922, he had evolved an esthetic principle which might be called "the discipline of double perception." The term is not quite exact, since the aim of double perception is ultimately a singleness of vision. This is the kind of vision everyone experiences when his two eyes, though each sees the same set of objects from slightly disparate angles, work together to produce a unified picture with a sense of

---

[9] Samuel Putnam, *op. cit.*, pp. 128-129.

depth to it. According to Hemingway, he was trying very hard for this double perception about the time of his return from the Near East in the fall of 1922. Aside from knowing "truly" what he "really" felt in the presence of any given piece of action, he found that his greatest difficulty lay in putting down on paper "what really happened in action; what the actual things were which produced the emotion" felt by the observer. No wonder that he was finding it hard to get "the real thing, the sequence of motion and fact which made the emotion." Whatever that real thing was, if you stated it "purely" enough and were likewise lucky, there was a chance that your statement of it would be valid, esthetically and emotionally valid, forever.[10]

Fundamental to the task is the deletion of one's own preconceptions. Such and such was the way it *ought* to be, the way you *assumed* it was. But "oughts" and "assumptions" are dangerous ground for a man to stand on who wishes to take the word of no one else, and to achieve in esthetics what René Descartes thought he had achieved in philosophy, namely, a start at the start. The hope was that the genuinely serious and determined writer-observer might be able in time to penetrate behind the illusions which all our preconceptions play upon the act of clear seeing.

It would then become his task to perfect himself in the discipline of double perception. To make something so humanly true that it will outlast the vagaries of time and change, yet will still speak directly to one's own changing time, he must somehow reach a state of objective awareness between two poles, one inward-outward and the other outward-inward. The first need (though not always first in order of time) is the ability to look within and to describe that complex of mixed emotions which a given set of circumstances has produced in the observer's mind. The other necessity is to locate and to state factually and exactly that outer complex of motion and fact which produced the emotional reaction.

This second class of things and circumstances, considered in their relations to the emotional complexes of the first class, would be precisely what T. S. Eliot called "objective correlatives."[11] His statement calls them variously "a set of objects, a situation, a chain of events which shall be the formula of that particular emotion; such that when the external facts, which must terminate in sensory experience, are given, the emotion is immediately

---

[10] *DIA*, p. 2.
[11] T. S. Eliot, *The Sacred Wood* (London, 1920), pp. 92-93.

evoked." He states further that the idea of artistic "inevitability" consists in the "complete adequacy of the external to the emotion." Mr. Eliot's generic description fits Hemingway's customary performance. Yet it may be noticed that Eliot's most frequent practice, as distinguished from his theoretical formulation, is to fashion his objective correlatives into a series of complex *literary* symbols. These are designed to elicit a more or less controlled emotional response from the reader (like the Wagnerian passage in *The Waste Land*), depending to some degree on the extent of his cultural holdings. With Hemingway, on the other hand, the objective correlatives are not so much inserted and adapted as observed and encompassed. They are to be traced back, not to anterior literature and art objects, but to things actually seen and known by direct experience of the world.

Hemingway's method has this special advantage over Eliot's— that one's ability to grasp the emotional suggestions embodied in an objective correlative depends almost solely on two factors: the reader's sensitivity to emotional suggestion, and the degree of his imaginative and sympathetic involvement in the story which is being told. With Eliot these two factors are likewise emphatically present, but a third is added. This third, which in a measure controls and delimits the first two, is the factor of "literary" experience. One's emotional response to the Wagnerian passage cannot be really full unless he knows its origin, can see it in both its original and its new and secondary context, and can make certain quick comparisons between the two. Some, though not all, of Eliot's correlatives accordingly show a "twice-removed" quality which in a measure pales and rarefies them. They cannot always achieve the full-bloodedness and immediacy of correlatives taken directly from the actual set of empirical circumstances which produced in the author the emotion which he is seeking to convey to the reader.

The objective correlatives in Hemingway appear to be of two main types, arbitrarily separable though always working together in a variety of ways. The first may be called *things-in-context:* that particular arrangement of facts in their relations to one another which constitutes a static field of perception. The second type may be called *things-in-motion*, since the arrangement of facts in their relations one to another is almost never wholly static. One might call any combination of the two types by the generic term of *what happened*, where the idea of happening implies a sequence of events in a certain order in time, though any event in the sequence can be arrested to form a static field of observation. If you have *what happened* in this special sense, you will have a chance of reproducing, in a perspective with depth, "the way it was."

To write for permanence, therefore, is to find and set down those things-in-context and things-in-motion which evoked a reaction in the writer as observer. Yet even the presence of both of these correlatives will not suffice to produce the total effect unless one also knows and says what he "really felt" in their presence. The important corollary idea of selection, meaning the elimination of the irrelevant and the unimportant at both poles, is clearly implied in Hemingway's phrase, "stated purely enough." During the five years of his early apprenticeship and the next five in which he developed his skills with such remarkable rapidity, the discipline of double perception was for Hemingway the leading esthetic principle. It is hard to imagine a better—or more difficult—task for the young writer to attempt. Although other principles and other skills have since arisen to complement and supplement this first one, it still occupies one whole side of his attention as an artist.

The basis of Hemingway's continuing power, and the real backbone of his eminence, is in practical esthetics. "Pure" or theoretical esthetics, of that special bloodless order which can argue to all hours without a glance at concretions, holds little interest for an artist of so pragmatic and empirical a cast of mind. One might even doubt that theoretical esthetics is of real interest to any genuine artist, unless in his alter ego he happens also to be a philosophical critic. If that is true, his artistic life is always in some danger, as Hemingway's is not. In esthetics as in his personal philosophy, he has labored hard to stay free of the wrong kind of illusion, and out from under the control of any cut-and-dried system, always trying instead to keep his eye trained on the thing in itself and the effect of the thing in himself. The actual, he wrote in 1949, is "made of knowledge, experience, wine, bread, oil, salt, vinegar, bed, early mornings, nights, days, the sea, men, women, dogs, beloved motor cars, bicycles, hills and valleys, the appearance and disappearance of trains on straight and curved tracks . . . cock grouse drumming on a basswood log, the smell of sweetgrass and fresh-smoked leather and Sicily."[12] Given the knowledge and experience of these and their unnamed equivalents, the artist can be at home in the world. If he is a practical esthetician whose aim

---

[12] Introd. to Elio Vittorino's novel, *In Sicily* (New York, 1949).

is to "invent truly," he is on firm ground. By experience he knows what will do. By observation he knows what will go—like the eminently practical Aristotle of the *Poetics*.

It was once remarked, though not by Aristotle, that the province of esthetics is the true and the beautiful, the province of morality the good. Of Hemingway as a moral writer there will be much to say. It is clear that the strongest conviction in Hemingway was the esthetician—the principle underlying his sense of place and fact and scene, the principle supporting his "discipline of double perception"—is the importance of telling truth.

Sheridan Baker

Jake Barnes and Spring Torrents

Nick Adams was soon to become Jake Barnes, as Hemingway mixed Paris into his war and alienation. He had continued to work daily, the most serious writer anyone seems to have known, a shy, cheerful, vigorous young man in sneakers and a jacket with one leathered elbow. He had an agreeable wife and "an infant son named Bumby who had been trained to put up his fists and assume a ferocious expression," one apparently "not as ferocious as his father would have liked," according to Harold Loeb's *The Way It Was.*

Loeb is the Robert Cohn of *The Sun Also Rises,* the first draft of which Hemingway wrote in a driving month and a half, directly after his friendship with Loeb exploded at the fiesta in Pamplona in July, 1925. Hemingway said that he had written "too fast each day to the point of complete exhaustion." After another three weeks he tossed off *The Torrents of Spring* in a little more than a week in November—after he "had finished the first draft of *The Sun Also Rises,* to cool out."

From *Ernest Hemingway: An Introduction and Interpretation* by Sheridan Baker, 40-55. Copyright © 1967 by Holt, Rinehart and Winston, Inc. Reprinted by permission of Holt, Rinehart and Winston, Inc.

The Torrents of Spring, like the more important book that caused
it, is an attack on former friends. It is chiefly a parody of Sherwood Anderson's *Dark Laughter*. Hemingway's first section is "Red
and Black Laughter," and a Negro's laugh echoes an Indian war
whoop at chapter endings. The title is from a novel by Turgenev,
whose *Sportsman's Sketches* Anderson admired as "the sweetest
thing in all literature," a book Jake Barnes had read more than
once, and one Hemingway later honored in the *Green Hills of Africa*
and in lists of recommended reading. Turgenev's *Torrents of Spring*
tells of love forsaken in springtime lust; and Hemingway remakes
Anderson's internal stirrings into a springtime thaw at a Petoskey
pump factory, leading Scripps O'Neil from one waitress to another
and then "out into the night, out into the night" (and the snow)
after a naked squaw. Occasionally the book is funny, and the
parody good: "Where had he been? Had he been in an Indian
club? What was it all about? Was this the end?" This does sound
like Anderson's interior tremolo; and making a surreptitious clubroom for Indians into a momentary wooden "Indian club" lifts
imitation into hilarity. Even better is a passage about hero O'Neil,
who has just sold a story to George Horace Lorimer (in actuality,
editor of *The Saturday Evening Post*, who name coincided happily
with that of Hemingway's own editor, Horace Liveright):

> Scripps striding through the Lake Country with Wordsworth. A field
> of golden daffodils. The wind blowing at Windermere. Far off, per-
> haps, a stag at bay. Ah, that was farther north, in Scotland. They
> were a hardy race, those Scots, deep in their mountain fastnesses.
> Harry Lauder and his pipe.

And more. There are moments of real hilarity concocted from the
literarily worn and false.

But the mixture is more often tasteless. Gertrude Stein comes
in for her helping. H. L. Mencken is coupled in the dedication
with S. Stanwood Menken, a true-blue American with whom con-
fusion was infuriating—but the jest smacks of expediency rather
than conviction. Hemingway indeed lacks conviction and indigna-
tion sufficient to sustain his highjinks. He quotes Fielding on the
Ridiculous, and either misses Fielding's point (that actuality fur-
ishes ample comedy) or cannot illustrate it—or thinks the statement itself is fusty and antique. He attempts a Fieldingesque
repartee with the reader, a poor thing not his own that is also to
muddle *Death in the Afternoon*. Though he could catch beautifully
the painful comedy of Nick's boyhood, though he could banter

nicely in private, as his letters show, though he could write un-
equaled dialogue that jests at scars and could sketch to perfection
the comic personality just off center-stage, he found the main show
deadly serious; and his Ridiculous becomes ridiculous.

Consequently, the self-parody frequently charged against Hemingway's weaker moments is sadly apparent in *The Torrents of
Spring*. Hemingway intends some of it, as in that hybrid of newspaper and creativity, Scripps O'Neil: Hemingway mocking himself
as a combination of the Scripps-Howard press and Eugene O'Neill.
And again, "Windermere" was the name of the Hemingways' summer home at Walloon Lake, a name chosen by Mrs. Hemingway
from her admired Sir Walter Scott. This fun is intentional. But
Hemingway's self-parody is also unintentional. The story is set in
Nick Adams's Michigan heartland, with coincidences of self-
mockery beyond anything Hemingway could have seen clearly.
Nick, too, loved a local waitress. Here again are the Indians (now
actually speaking of the White Father and Manitou) and the
Peerless tobacco and the railroad tracks of Hemingway's high-
school story. Here is the wounded veteran inhibited from sexual
intercourse and troubled—a cooling out of Jake Barnes indeed.
He is another Krebs, who wants to talk about the war and cannot
convey the truth of it: two Indian veterans, who do not need to
talk about it, doubt that Yogi Johnson was even in it. And Hemingway, no longer comic, seems to bloody the facts as much as "that
fellow Anderson" had made them pallid: "Most of the men he had
known had been excited as hell when they had first killed. The
trouble was to keep them from killing too much." With Yogi
Johnson we are momentarily in Hemingway's private hell, where
the truth always comes out the color of fiction, and the fiction
always colors the truth.

And here is the Hemingway prose, which he cannot help writing
as he parodies styles too near his own: "There were a pile of deer
shipped down by hunters from the Upper Peninsula of Michigan,
lying piled the one on the other, dead and stiff and drifted half
over with snow on the station platform." Omit the slight parodic
inflation (beginning with "shipped" and running through "the one
on the other"), and we are indeed "In Another Country"—to be
written sometime after March the next year: "There was much
game hanging outside the shops, and the snow powdered in the fur
of the foxes and the wind blew their tails. The deer hung stiff and
heavy and empty, and small birds blew in the wind and the wind
turned their feathers." Hemingway cannot keep from writing like
himself. The Indian clubroom has real moments; the drummer in

the beanery is Hemingway at his incidental best. But the book itself is an embarrassment.

The *Torrents* cooled Hemingway off, at the expense of former friends, and at his own expense: hysteria vaguely lurks behind the hilarity, as it was later effectively to do in Nick's mad talk of grasshoppers, in "A Way You'll Never Be." Somewhere uneasily in the background is Hemingway's narcissistic obsession, Hemingway vaguely picking at himself in the dark, Hemingway attacking as untrue the art he is making out of his own shadows, and punishing himself for distorting into fiction the personal truth he cannot locate, a faint foreshadowing of the final untrue self-disgust that led to suicide.

The Sun Also Rises had also begun as an attack on a former friend and also represents a considerable measure of self-punishment. Hemingway had met Harold Loeb in the fall of 1923 at one of Ford Madox Ford's weekly teas, and Loeb had then sought out his friendship. His mother was a Guggenheim; his father, of the family famous for the Loeb Classical Library. Harold Loeb was now the rich young angel of a New York little magazine, and had a novel nearly finished. Soon he and Hemingway were playing tennis, boxing between sets, dining together, playing bridge, talking about writing.

In August, 1924, Liveright accepted Loeb's *Doodab*. In September, Hemingway and Loeb "made plans for skiing that winter in Austria, trout fishing in the spring on a very special Spanish river, and then going on to the bullfights in Pamplona." In October, Hemingway and Loeb went to Senlis, where, over a long, murderous two-man poker game in the hotel room, Hemingway's antagonism momentarily broke out.

Very soon, after a dozen oysters and two bottles of wine, Loeb, the successful novelist, presumed to advise his friend about writing. Hemingway needed to put in some women, Loeb said, suggesting that Hemingway's happy marriage had robbed him of necessary misery. Again Hemingway flared, and then told of his lost "English" nurse in Milan. Next, Loeb took Hemingway to meet Leon Fleischman, with whom Loeb had just signed his Liveright contract. Hemingway disliked him at once but sent him the *In Our Time* manuscript. In December, the Hemingways and party went skiing in Austria, Loeb promising to follow after settling the editorial affairs of *Doodab*.

From Austria, Hemingway wrote Loeb wishing he were there and asking him to get his book back from Fleischman: he had learned that Donald Ogden Stewart had sent another version of it to the Doran company. But the book had already gone to New York. Loeb decided to sail for New York himself to settle his own editorial questions and perhaps to help out good old Hem. And indeed he did. He dropped into Liveright's just in time to persuade the manuscript reader to give *In Our Time* another reading. When it was accepted by Liveright, Loeb cabled Hemingway in Austria. On February 27, 1925, Hemingway got Loeb's cable and a similar one from Stewart (now also interceding with Liveright). Hemingway immediately wrote Loeb his thanks and many questions, particularly asking if his book would make fall publication along with Loeb's. He returned to Paris elated, only to be piqued again when Loeb told him of the rescue. Anderson too had claimed an assist, as did Stewart, and now Loeb. It looked as if he needed help from half of New York.

In the spring, Bill Smith, Hemingway's boyhood summer friend in Michigan, arrived. He and Loeb became friends, matching Hemingway and Paul Fisher at tennis, dining together when Hemingway, the married man, had to leave for home. The Hemingways had already met Lady Duff Twysden (Loeb makes it "Twitchell"), a tweedy British Circe, and her lover, Pat Guthrie (Loeb's "Swazey"). It was Paris in the spring. Spain and fishing and Pamplona were just ahead. And the cast of *The Sun Also Rises* had gathered.

Then in June, Harold Loeb slipped off to St.-Jean-de-Luz with Duff Twysden. The rich young Jew, the Princeton man, Coach Spider Kelly's shining bantam with the handsomely flattened nose, who could outplay Hemingway at tennis and outbox his twitching eye, who had beaten him to publication and then had too fortunately helped him—had run off with the most desirable woman in Paris. Hemingway was certainly jealous, and certainly in love with her, though Duff's friendly respect for Hadley seems to have kept him at a pleasantly miserable distance.

Loeb stayed on at St.-Jean-de-Luz after Duff went back to Pat Guthrie, just back from a mission to London and mother for money. Hemingway asked them to come along on the fishing and bullfighting party. Duff and Pat decided to stay in St.-Jean-de-Luz until time for the fights, Loeb, hoping for another chance, wired that he too would skip the fishing and would meet Hemingway in Pamplona on Monday, July 6, 1925.

The St.-Jean-de-Luz threesome was far from happy. Guthrie was jealous; Duff had arrived wearing not her usual slouched hat but a beret on the Hemingway pattern; and Loeb was uneasy about his *coup de boudoir* and the evident complications with Hemingway. The three drove to Pamplona on Sunday, July 5.

For Hemingway, Hadley, Bill Smith, and Donald Stewart, the fishing had gone sour. Hemingway's editor had delayed their start (June 24 or 25); a new reservoir had spoiled their stream. They had caught nothing. They arrived in Pamplona on Monday, July 6, 1925. But spirits revived after drinks and lunch. Everyone went to watch the bulls unloaded, and the fiesta was on.

Tuesday morning, Hemingway, Smith, and Loeb tried the crowded amateur cowfighting (with the Amazonian cows of the fighting breed, as it would seem from Loeb's pictures and Hemingway's explanation in *Death in the Afternoon.*) Then came a day of fights with Hemingway enthusiastic about Cayetano Ordonez, Niño de la Palma. Next morning Hemingway, Smith, and Loeb again tried the amateur run. Loeb, turning to save himself, rode across the arena seated between the cow's horns, to be tossed in the air and to land on his feet. Smith made one good pass with his jacket and received one butting. Hemingway grabbed a cow's horns from behind and bulldogged her to the ground to the crowd's delight. New York photographers caught Loeb and Smith in action, but missed Hemingway, except once as background. Hemingway had already met Niño de la Palma, who spoke with amused admiration of Loeb's (not Hemingway's) bullfighting. Loeb seemed to be upstaging him at every turn.

Thursday, July 9, brought the explosion. On Wednesday after dinner, Hadley had gone to her room with a headache, and Hemingway with her. Guthrie wandered off. Loeb and Duff Twysden went off for a quiet drink, which led to someone's party and eventually to Loeb dead drunk and Duff off on the town. She came to lunch on Thursday with a black eye and a bruised forehead. For the afternoon fights, Duff and Guthrie moved up to sit with the Hemingways, and Smith and Stewart moved down with Loeb. Dinner was silent and strained. Then Hemingway began to needle Loeb about his coolness toward bullfighting. Guthrie joined in. Until finally:

"Look here," said Pat. "I may be dumb. I may be useless. But I know enough to stay away when I'm not wanted."

"Is that how you got through school?" [asked Loeb.]

"You lay off Pat," said Hem grimly. "You've done enough to spoil this party."

They told Loeb to get out. Loeb said he would "the instant Duff wants it." Duff said she did not want it. "You lousy bastard," said Hemingway. "Running to a woman." Loeb then invited Hemingway out. They walked solemnly toward a dark corner. Loeb was afraid, he remembers, because he knew he could not outbox a big and angry Hemingway. He also knew their friendship was over:

> I was tremendously sad—so sad that for a moment I forgot to be afraid. It was my pattern, I felt, slowly, gradually, to acquire a friend and then have him turn in an instant into a bitter, lashing enemy. It had happened at Princeton and Mohegan, and in The Sunwise Turn [his bookshop]. Even in marriage. There was something about me. I felt excruciatingly lonely . . . .

Loeb put his glasses in his jacket and looked for a safe place to hang it. "Shall I hold it for you?" grinned Hemingway, and the battle was off.

Everyone pretended that nothing had happened. Hemingway put a heartfelt apology in Loeb's box. They stayed through the fiesta (from July 7 to 11, by Hemingway's calendar in *Death in the Afternoon*). On the last day Niño de la Palma earned the bull's ear and presented it to Hadley; and he and the Hemingways left for Madrid. In *Death in the Afternoon* (1932), Hemingway remembers:

> Hadley, with the bull's ear wrapped in a handkerchief, the ear was very stiff and dry and the hair all wore off it and the man who cut the ear is bald now too and slicks long strips of hair over the top of his head and he was a beau then. He was, all right.

Duff, Guthrie, Smith, and Loeb drove back to St.-Jean-de-Luz together.

Ten days later in Valencia, on July 21, 1925, his twenty-sixth birthday, Hemingway started *The Sun Also Rises*. He wrote through the rest of July and all of August, in Valencia, Madrid, St. Sebastian, and Hendaye, following the fights, and vacationing where Jake Barnes is to vacation. He finished the first draft in Paris on September 6, 1925. He relaxed for the rest of September, then turned to *The Torrents of Spring*. He went to ski in Austria for the rest of November and December. He started rewriting *The Sun Also Rises* in January, 1926, and took a trip to New York in February. By the end of March he had finished, cutting almost a third (40,000 words) of his first draft. Scribner's published it on October 22, 1926.

The Sun Also Rises starts as a satirical portrait of Robert Cohn, who sees the world as W. H. Hudson's *Purple Land* and the abandoned Brett as "absolutely fine and straight." The portrait is penetrating, sympathetic, and scandalously close to the details of Loeb's life, exactly catching the plaintive romantic whom Loeb reveals in his own book, the pathetic good guy with "a nice, boyish sort of cheerfulness that had never been trained out of him." Loeb actually speaks of Hudson's South America, and thinks of the fallen woman as an angel with the voice of a bird. Loeb confesses his gift for irritating people with his need for friendship and recognition, and with his non-Hemingway incidence of good luck. On his high escapade with Duff Twysden, he drew a perfect bridge hand. "You *would* get thirteen hearts," she said. She told him that she was not sure he belonged to her "esoteric circle." Discussing the Hemingways, she said that perhaps Loeb was "not one of us after all."

This is indeed Cohn of *The Sun Also Rises*, the outsider so earnestly wanting in. Brett repeatedly tells Jake that Count Mippipopolous is "one of us"; and it is clear that Cohn is not. He is not an *aficionado*. *Afición*, the freemasonry of bullfighting, can excuse almost any defect. Montoya, the hotelkeeper immediately forgives Barnes his tourist friends: "Without his ever saying anything they were simply a little something shameful between us, like the spilling open of the horses in bullfighting." So it is with the defects within the Paris group—Brett's infidelities, Mike's weaknesses, Harvey Stone's drink—a little shameful but within the esoteric circle of the lost, a circle that inexorably excludes Cohn, the unrealist still living by Victorian mottoes, springing to arms over imaginary insults to a nonexistent lady, trying to be well lost but never making it.

By the beginning of the third chapter, Jake Barnes's attention has shifted from Robert Cohn to himself:

> It was a warm spring night and I sat at a table on the terrace of the Napolitain after Robert had gone, watching it get dark and the electric signs come on, and the red and green stop-and-go traffic-signal, and the crowd going by, and the horse-cabs clippety-clopping along at the edge of the solid taxi traffic, and the *poules* going by, singly and in pairs, looking for the evening meal.

The slow attractive dirge on being lost and doomed has begun. Barnes picks up a sour little prostitute "because of a vague sentimental idea that it would be nice to eat with some one," excusing himself from sexual intercourse on the grounds that he is "sick." "Everybody's sick," says the girl. Jake's peculiar wistfulness, a poetic hyperbole of everybody's sickness, is soon explained: the war has left him a sexual cripple, incapable of ever escaping from loneliness into consummated love.

"You are all a lost generation," said Gertrude Stein to Hemingway; and he took her sentence as his epigraph, together with an old echo from Ecclesiastes—which, he stated much later, was intended as a refutation of lostness: "One generation passeth away, and another generation cometh; but the earth abideth forever. . . . The sun also ariseth, and the sun goeth down, and hasteth to the place where he arose. . . ." But to say that the sun *also* rises is to emphasize that it has set. The sun also rises, yes, and the earth abides, yes; but our generation is no longer here to rise nor to stay; and the ancient classical sadness of this fact echoes Biblically and beautifully underneath everything in Barnes's meditation on the past, underneath the bright moments, the happiness of getting away from it all with a sound friend, the pleasures of countryside and fiesta and bullfight.

Jake Barnes represents the best of the lost generation, the best that is lost. Barnes is the maimed knight of the lost. As Mark Spilka suggests, in his "The Death of Love in *The Sun Also Rises*," Barnes is uncomfortably similar to Cohn, the romantic knight in full flower; and he is sadly incapable of the self-sufficient manhood of Romero, the bullfighter, who has drawn the sportsman's independent contest to a point of steely beauty in spite of the wasted world. Jake is powerless between the two, in spite of a decent stoicism in a lost world, with a decent community of lost spirit and a measure of existential courage for getting on with a bad job.

His crowd is not only a generation lost: it has lost its powers of generation in turn. It is lost from the succession of generations on which the sun will rise and set and rise again. Barnes is a newspaperman, an ex-aviator made impotent by war, wounded in a way usually considered comic while "flying on a joke front like the Italian." Sent to recuperate in England, he has met Lady Brett Ashley, a member of the Voluntary Aid Detachment of amateur nurses and helpers. They have fallen in love and tried some sort of consummation: "I don't want to go through that hell again," says Brett, who still cannot keep from seeing him. Jake's wound has wounded her too, and helped to turn her into the siren of Paris and Pamplona.

Now it is Paris, 1924.[1] Jake is living alone, working hard, treating himself and the world with decent irony and pity—as Bill Gorton is to recommend ironically—except that it "is awfully easy to be hard-boiled about everything in the daytime, but at night it is another thing." He looks at his maimed self in the mirror, placed *à la mode* beside the bed. He turns out the light. His head "starts to work." Once, for six months he had "never slept with the electric light off."

Jake is, of course, another Lieutenant Nick, who lays him down but cannot sleep, the crippled hero able to pray only in a hopeless way, a Catholic knowing that the Church is right in its advice to forget one's self, but knowing that it is impossible to do so, hoping that someday he will be a better Catholic but knowing that there is really no hope. Like Nick, Jake is one whom the civilized world and its wars have cut away from their generations, the essential motherless child of conflagration, the young man without woman ("To hell with women, anyway. To hell with you, Brett Ashley").

Hemingway's persistent exclusion of his own marriage from the adolescent heartland of rod and gun and mountain air emphasizes the callow yearning of his masculine ideality. While actually skiing with his wife and others, he writes of two young men skiing alone against the shadow of a pregnant wife somewhere else. Following an unsuccessful fishing trip with his wife and others, he writes a masculine idyl of wood and stream. Following a fiesta with his wife, and a trip to Madrid with his wife and the bullfighter they had befriended, he writes an idyl about the Belle Dame sans Merci and a male beautifully and sadly inside the magic circle because impotent and now forever invulnerable, and forever lost.

The energy in the book comes directly from this magic spring. Hemingway, working so close to the facts of Loeb, Twysden, and Pamplona as almost to seem mere journalist, has touched a primal pulsation of mythology: the unearthly and unquenchable mythic appeal of the sorceress who, in spite of herself and with a regretful sigh, must emasculate the men she attracts. The romantic Cohn calls Brett Ashley a Circe who "turns men into swine," an idea scorned as literary by the inner circle of realists; but Hemingway

---

[1] Dated by Romero's age and birth year, and oddly authenticated by mention of Charles Ledoux—Ch. IX—who forfeited his European featherweight title on June 25, 1924, by refusing a challenge; for this nonexistent fight, Hemingway supplies a fictional opponent, apparently a version of the "Ad Francis" in "The Battler." Hemingway has apparently placed his story a year earlier than the actual events as part of the fictional disguise.

plays along with the British expression "swine" through several succeeding pages, and Brett becomes the goddess of the wild fiesta that wrecks all their relationships except that of the two impotent lovers, the sorceress and her victim. Jake sees Brett through the crowd "walking, her head up, as though the fiesta were being staged in her honor, and she found it pleasant and amusing." Earlier, some dancers in wreaths of garlic have put her inside their circle: "They wanted her as an image to dance around"; after the dance they rush her to a wineshop and enthrone her on a cask. The friends pick up the humor and "translate" her to the hotel like a holy image.

Hemingway may simply be reporting; he certainly is not attempting any elaborate mythical parallel. But the mythical tracings are there, and extend through the whole book. Mike has "behaved badly" and, in Brett's words, has been "a swine." Jake says that everyone behaves badly with the proper chance. "You wouldn't behave badly," says Brett. And Jake is indeed ultimately decent, the crippled Catholic among pagans: he first slips into swinedom in the baiting of Cohn and is disgusted with his satisfaction in it. Jake remains the paragon of the lost. Bill Gorton, who at first seems a steady center, able, sympathetic, but above the battle, slips into swine-calling companionship with Mike (against previous victims of Mike's sponging), only to have Mike sponge on him at last: "Bill's face sort of changed." In the end, it is the emasculate Jake who rescues the lady in distress, as he and she silently knew he would—Jake, wiser and sadder because he knows he can behave badly and can betray the fellowship of bullfighting by pandering for his siren, a steer leading the bull to the slaughter.

For Circe must emasculate her lovers: unman them into caricatures of the lust that took their manhood, swine forever beneath her favors. Brett is not all Circe, of course; Hemingway simply works out the paradigm of siren and emasculation from his own private preoccupations. But like Circe, Brett must have an ever new man to replace the ones she drains.

Looking lovely, she sees the palm of Romero's bullfighting hand potent of "thousands of bulls." She has previously responded to a bull's power, looking down at "the great hump of muscle on his neck swollen tight": "My God, isn't he beautiful?" Jake and his friends are uncomfortably aware that Jake is a steer, making accidental references as they try to overlook it. Emasculation dins sadly through the book from Jake's whim with the prostitute onward. "Must be swell being a steer," says Bill, as Jake explains the herding of bulls by docile steers doomed to be hurt—exactly Jake's eventual function, herding the bullfighter in for Brett. "Why do you follow Brett around like a poor bloody steer?" Mike shouts at Cohn; and, as Spilka has noted, we are reminded that this is what Jake too, in painful literalness, is also doing. "Tell him bulls have no balls," shouts drunken Mike at the bullfighter, trying to drive him away from Brett. And when Don Manuel Orquito attempts to launch his fire balloons, we have a pathetic symbol of the whole fiesta from Jake's emasculate point of view: "The people shouted as each new luminous paper bubble careened, caught fire, and fell." "Globos illuminados," Mike said. "A bunch of bloody globos illuminados."

Testicles and the lack of testicles—an idea Hemingway consistently associates with bullfighting, using the Spanish slang *cojones* —are clearly symbols of power and failure in *The Sun Also Rises*. Nevertheless, Hemingway was to say in his interview with George Plimpton thirty years later:

> Who ever said Jake was "emasculated precisely as is a steer"? Actually he had been wounded in quite a different way and his testicles were intact and not damaged. Thus he was capable of all normal feelings as a *man* but incapable of consummating them. The important distinction is that his wound was physical and not psychological and that he was not emasculated.

But whatever Hemingway's private picture of Jake's disfigurement and however that picture may have changed over the years, the similarity of Jake's deprivation to that of a steer is too insistent to be set aside. To be sure, Hemingway's later description of Jake as a man with no penis uncovers a horror in the Hemingway imagination of which there is much veiled evidence in his work and in anecdotes of his own lacks and sensitivities.[1] This picture of Jake would fit the evidence of the book, with the references to steers simply touching a general symbology too close for comfort. Jake remains a man, as Hemingway says, with normal feelings but with crippled capability, living with perpetual frustration.

The story of Jake Barnes is really one of education: "Perhaps as you went along you did learn something. I did not care what it was all about. All I wanted to know was how to live in it." How to live in a shattered world is Jake's problem, and he is educated

---

[1] See Hemingway's fury at Max Eastman's apparent reference to inches in Loeb, *The Way It Was* (p. 252).

to the reality of just how lost his generative island with its Circe really is, awakening finally on the cold hillside. Jake is educated to its ruin, and to his own, as he slowly changes from the man who keeps asking Brett if they can't "do something about it" to the man who can say to Brett's final wish as to how nice it might have been between them: "Yes, . . . Isn't it pretty to think so?" Spilka has well pointed out the nature of Barnes's education, his final realization that, even without his wound, he and Brett would be cases of arrested development, canceled out of the scheme of generation in a world where love and religion seem defunct, the two of them put in their places by Romero, who is living cleanly and manfully in a dangerous world and paying the bill. It never could have been nice between Jake and Brett. Jake has finally seen the distinction between this lost world as it is, in which one can have none of the dreams, and that romantic world where lovers live happily ever after. He has seen himself betray Romero into the siren's arms, and felt the scorn of Montoya; he knows that there is nothing left but to play the impotent knight to his fatal lady, the helplessly deceitful steer.

Brett, too, is educated to the truth of lost generation. She has found her match in the virile killer of bulls, the "lovely boy" fifteen years her junior. He breaks her, in effect, in her only fragility: "Brett was radiant . . . . 'I feel altogether changed . . . .'" The bullfighter has almost changed the siren into a woman, breaking her with self-realization at last. She refuses him, of course: "I'm thirty-four, you know. I'm not going to be one of those bitches that ruins children." She is too old, already out of the scheme of generation. She realizes indirectly, that she, who has seemed a super-woman, is not even completely a woman at all. The bullfighter has thought her not womanly enough. Her hair is short and boyish. She remains a personification (as indeed she seems almost to have been in real life) of sex without responsibility, the male dream fulfilled, the everlasting initial female, the siren. She realizes that she too is impotent, one of the lost: "I can't even marry Mike," she says, in her moment of truth. And the book ends with the two impotent lovers, just touching as the taxi jounces, thinking how nice it might have been—or at least how pretty to think so.

As both Spilka and Carlos Baker (in his *Hemingway, the Writer as Artist*) have noticed in different ways, *The Sun Also Rises* is a species of chivalric romance after all, in its very demolition of the romantic dream. As Spilka says, Hemingway's protagonists "are deliberately shaped as allegorical figures"; and one measure of that shaping is Hemingway's giving Brett the illusion, apparently not in her actual counterpart's mind, that she and Mike would someday marry. One dream falls, but a still sweeter romantic agony remains. "It might have been"—no sweeter words of tongue or pen—continues to shimmer over the ruins left by "never could have been." This is the force behind the siren's cry. As the troubadours knew, the real sweetness of love is its unfulfillment. Hemingway has written the courtly romance for moderns, tough, dissonant, yet echoing forever the ancient sweetness of being forever lovelorn and forever longing, all underlined by the final knowledge of damnation, knowing that it never could have been, yet doomed to think that it might.

Hemingway's persistent yet buried self-pity has at last turned to the great romantic subject of love. He has amusingly come around to the very advice with which Harold Loeb had so infuriated him— to put women into his writing—including not only Loeb's own Lady Duff, but also something of the nurse, of whom he then told Loeb, who threw him into the agony of hopeless longing, the central romantic passion and the buried center of *The Sun Also Rises*, the nurse about whom he had already written "A Very Short Story" and would soon write *A Farewell to Arms*.

"It might have been" echoes sweetly and painfully beneath everything Jake Barnes thinks and does, made resonant by his admirably tough and stoic surface, even after we close the book on his final acceptance of his emotional and moral impotence. How nice it might have been to have picked up a companionable girl, and dined and drunk and bedded. How nice to have found comfort in the Church. How nice to have been with Brett from start to finish, to have done what Cohn had done. How nice, in the beautiful fishing interlude, if one could really get away, and get away from women, and make it last, and fish with Bill and the lonely Harris again. How nice to be a boy with a girl on a raft. And, yes, at the end, how nice to be safely lost and a good consort to the lost —two together in a bar, with a polite and efficient bartender, and the perfect martini and the olive.

There it is, and there it will always be: the troubadour of the roaring twenties catching the beautiful and the damned, with irony and pity, in the delicious chill of the iced glass, the quiet moment for two, aware of the sweet sad glow before the fraying of the dream. He has really outdone his friend Fitzgerald. *The Sun Also Rises* is a wonderful book because it hits so deadly center the pathetic and unadmirable wish that will not die, the pleasure in wishful unfulfillment, the pleasure in pitying ourselves for not getting what we think we deserve. And the pity carries over into what Vergil called "the tears of things," as Hemingway's stream of sensuousness (in *Time* magazine's phrase) carries us along, the bell-like Biblical and classical sadness in the fact that for us the things of this world must pass, even though the sun can rise again. The sad wonder of life flows before us, caught as it was at the moment, never to return but always to be.

Things stay in the reader's mind: the girl looking absently away from her boxing puppets, "the sad tables of the Rotonde," the Basque cutting off a stream of wine with his teeth, the spat of rope-soled shoes dancing, the craftsman jumping on his wineskins to prove them sound, barges on the river, mountains with aged beech trees and "smooth grass, very green and fresh." Yet, strangely, Hemingway is not a sensuous writer. There is no metaphorical packing and no reticulated detail to help us see and feel distinctly. All is understated; all is bare outline. The reader is surprised at how much he himself is importing to fill it out. Hemingway picks the detail that calls forth the nod:

> After a while we came out of the mountains, and there were trees along both sides of the road, and a stream and ripe fields of grain, and the road went on, very white and straight ahead, and then lifted to a little rise, and off on the left was a hill with an old castle, with buildings close around it and a field of grain going right up to the walls and shifting in the wind. I was up in front with the driver and I turned around. Robert Cohn was asleep, but Bill looked and nodded his head.

The general outlines, which Carlos Baker has likened to those of the eighteenth century, ask from us the understanding nod we are flattered to be asked to give: simply "an old castle," which we immediately complete with whatever we need and know. The general idea and the bare hint sufficies our worldly knowledge, in secret collusion with the author.

The clipped essentiality of the dialogue, frequently and justly admired, operates in much the same way. The characters themselves are understaters, and we get their understatement further selected for sharp illustration, the detail of idiom caught alive, full of momentary quip and amusement, and full of instant revelations of character:

"Are you a sadist, Brett? I asked.

"Hope not."

"He said Brett was a sadist just because she has a good, healthy stomach."

"Won't be healthy long."

Or Mike, wishing Cohn were in jail for knocking him down:

"Oh, no," said Edna. "You don't mean that."

"I do, though," Mike said. "I'm not one of these chaps likes being knocked about. I never play games, even."

Mike took a drink.

"I never liked to hunt, you know. There was always the danger of having a horse fall on you . . . ."

Even the superb, hurt chatter of Frances is finally reduced to suggestion only, as Jake can stand no more and looks back through a window:

Frances was talking on to him, smiling brightly, looking into his face each time she asked: "Isn't it so, Robert?" Or maybe she did not ask that now. Perhaps she said something else.

The truth for which Hemingway strove is perhaps never more sharply achieved, though we may wish that he had made up more of it, as he shaped it into myth. The book reads and rereads with a flow of sharp perceptions which, even without documentation, we know come from the very life. The hard surface allows us to indulge our romantic self-pity in secret, to be, with Jake Barnes, tough and decent in spite of our failings, and to imagine ourselves beautifully damned by a world unworthy of us. We read with pleasure, in silent collusion with Hemingway, *aficionados* with a slight consciousness of a little something shameful between us, like the spilling out of the horses in bullfighting.

James T. Farrell

The Sun Also Rises

Ernest Hemingway's first novel, *The Sun Also Rises*, has been generally heralded as the definitive account of a war wearied lost generation. In the light of this interpretation it is interesting to note that this novel was published in 1926, and that the time of its action is 1925. For these years fall within the most hopeful period of the post-Versailles world.

At that time there were many signs (at least in the eyes of superficial observers) to suggest that the world was returning to normalcy. After 1923, European capitalism seemed to have been restabilized, following the shocks of war, revolution, and dangers of revolution. At least to some, Germany looked like a going concern: the Weimar Republic was considered firmly secure. Hope was being revived in cartels as the means of achieving peaceable allocation of markets and equitable access to sources of raw materials. The epoch of disarmament talks, peace pacts, peace conferences had begun. America was in the full sweep of a tremendous economic boom, leading many to believe that this country was

From *The New York Times* (August 1, 1943). © 1943 by The New York Times Company. Reprinted by permission of the New York Times Company and the author.

paving the way toward a new era of unprecedented world prosperity.

It may seem paradoxical that in such a period a novel of war
disillusionment, nihilistic in outlook, should have become an international success.

However, this paradox is only superficial. With signs of a return
to world prosperity there were growing evidences of pacifism. In
particular, the youth which had been too young to have been in
the trenches was deeply pacifistic. Disillusionment with the war
was more or less accepted. In addition, a re-examination of the
character of disillusionment portrayed in *The Sun Also Rises* suggests that this mood had become a way of feeling and acting; in
fact, a social habit. By 1925 those who had been morally unhinged
or physically maimed during the war had had a number of years in
which to make some kind of adjustment to the postwar world. The
period of the first difficult readjustment had passed. Such, for
instance, is the case of the chief protagonist in *The Sun Also Rises*.
Jake Barnes, impotent as a result of wounds suffered on the
Italian front, has more or less reconciled himself to his condition.

Whenever there is a widespread mood of disillusionment caused
by an event as catastrophic as a world war, that mood is bound to
be nihilistic and rather adolescent in character unless it serves as
the basis for a radical and progressive political orientation that
aims to change and better the world. This is illustrated in *The Sun
Also Rises*.

The characters express their bitterness, their feelings of disen-
chantment, with calculated bravado. Their conversation is reduced
to enthusiastic small talk about their escapades. And this talk, as
well as their actions, is largely a matter of pose and gesture. They
act like people who have not fully grown up and who lack the self-
awareness to realize this; in fact, they possess no desire to grow up.

The Sun Also Rises influenced younger persons more widely
than it did members of Hemingway's own generation. He may
have reflected the feelings of many who fought in the war; but most
of these men were finding some way of settling down and adjusting
themselves in the nineteen-twenties. Some were doing creative
writing, some finding editorial jobs, some launching themselves in
careers that later won them Pulitzer prizes in poetry and so on. This
novel struck deeper chords in the youth of the Twenties.

Hemingway's first books had hardly been published when he had
imitators all over America; furthermore, boys and girls on campus
after campus began to talk like Hemingway characters. One need

not go into detail to describe certain features of the Twenties; these are too fresh in our minds. Suffice it to say that by and large younger people were revolting against the standards and conventions of their elders, against the accepted notions of middle-class society. At the same time they were nonpolitical in their revolt. Add to this the deep pacificism of the decade, and one can easily understand why this novel struck such chords of response among young people, why Hemingway suddenly became the influence he did become at the time.

His influence was not merely superficial. It played a liberating and salutary role on those who would become the next generation of writers, and, more so, numerically, on readers. The hopes of those days have now been proved a snare by history. The nihilistic character of Hemingway's writing helped to free younger people from these false hopes. And although this novel (and many of his early stories as well) is set against a European background, Hemingway helped focus the eyes of younger people sharply on American life.

His writing was exciting and possessed of an extraordinary power of suggestiveness; it won over the reader to the feeling that he was actually participating in the lives of very real men and women. His use of dialogue helped enormously to create this impression. Others, notably Ring Lardner, preceded Hemingway in exploring and revealing the literary possibilities of the use of American vernacular, but he used it with amazing skill and originality. Both his suggestiveness in conveying a sense of life and his use of dialogue tended to turn the attention of youth toward common American experiences and to the speech expressing them on city streets and farms.

But Hemingway's influence, though so widespread, at the same time has been one that seems quickly to have exhausted itself. For Hemingway is a writer of limited vision, one who has no broad and fertile perspective on life. Younger writers were influenced—even seduced—by his moods; and they could grasp from him a sense of the great possibilities to be discovererd in the true and simple treatment of common subject matter and in the use of ordinary speech. But once they had learned these lessons, they could gain little more from Hemingway.

The Europe described in *The Sun Also Rises* is a tourist's Europe of the Twenties. Cafés, restaurants, hotels, particularly of the Left Bank, are the setting. When the action shifts to Spain, it is to permit a magnificent description of bull fights and a fiesta. The mood and attitude of the main characters is that of people on a vacation. They set out to do what people want to do on a vacation: they have love affairs, they drink, go fishing, and see new spectacles. Written in the first person, the book unfolds from the standpoint of a spectator's attitude. Jake, the narrator, is a newspaper man; his is an occupation that naturally tends to develop the point of view of the spectator. Jake is constantly looking at the other characters, at himself, at the scenery of Spain, at the bull fight, at everything that occurs or comes within his view.

The main characters have only a meager past. They are escaping from their past and usually do not wish even to talk or to think of it. They live for the present, constantly searching for new and fresh sensations. They do not really think; even Jake scarcely thinks about himself or about his own impotence. These people feel quite alike. They form a small clique, stoically accepting the ills of their life.

Robert Cohn, however, is an outsider. He is with them because of his doglike love for Lady Brett Ashley. Unlike the others, he is unable to drown his feelings in banalities, small talk, and new spectacles. Cohn's difference from the others is one of the central points of the novel. This contrast is stated overtly when Lady Brett says that Cohn is "not one of us," and when Jake thinks that Cohn has behaved badly by pursuing Lady Brett. Focused against Cohn, Jake's simple, stoical attitude is enforced more strongly. The attitude of Jake is one of the basic attitudes in Hemingway's writings.

Hemingway's realism is, by and large, one which deals with sensations—with shocks to the senses. He has tended to reduce life to the effect that sights, scenes, and experiences make upon the nervous system; and he has avoided complicated types of response. Herein we find one of the major factors revealing his limitations as a writer.

In his most representative work he has saved himself from the crudities of simple behaviorism because of his gift of suggestiveness and his developed skill of understatement. The moral outlook in his work is on a plane of equal simplicity with his characters and subject matter. It amounts to the attitude that an action is good if it makes one feel good. Such an outlook on characters and events suggests that a development of greater understanding—broader range of feeling and sympathy, greater depth of imagination—is practically precluded.

This has been the case in Hemingway's career. He arrived on the literary scene absolute master of the style he has made his own; his attitudes were firmly fixed at that time. And he said pretty much what he had to say with his first stories and his first two novels.

As a novelist, it is my opinion that the best of Ernest Hemingway is still to be found in *The Sun Also Rises*. Its freshness has not faded with time. It remains one of the very best American novels of the Twenties.

Earl Rovit

The Sun Also Rises: An
Essay in Applied Principles

The Sun Also Rises (1926), Hemingway's first and perhaps most completely successful novel, is best discussed in isolation from any thematic or technical concerns. It is, in many ways, an anomalous work in Hemingway's lifetime of publication: it is characteristic Hemingway; yet it is an uncharacteristic Hemingway fiction. It was written partly out of a disgust with the empty Bohemianism of "The Lost Generation," but it has served to make that Bohemianism eminently attractive to succeeding generations of readers. It was read originally as a *roman à cléf* in which the major (and some of the minor) characters could be identified by those with the inside knowledge; time has made some of these very characters secure, living fictional beings.

Hemingway has insisted that *The Sun Also Rises* is a tragedy and not a "hollow or bitter satire," but criticism has been slow to accept either of his definitions. In fact, although it seems to me that some of the best of Hemingway criticism has concerned itself with this novel, there is a surprising lack of unanimity

From *Ernest Hemingway,* Twayne's United States Authors, No. 41 (New York: Twayne, 1963), 147-162. Copyright 1963 by Twayne Publishers. Reprinted by permission of the publishers.

among critics on what would seem to be basic non-controversial issues. Critics have divided handsomely on determining where the moral center of the book rests; some have found it in Pedro Romero, some in Jake Barnes, and there have even been spirited defenses of Robert Cohn. There have been attempts to read the book as an elegy on the death of love, and others to show that the sun does rise out of the wasteland.

When good critics disagree so violently, we can assume that there must be much smoke and much fire also, and that the novel must rest on a special base of ambiguity. Therefore I offer my reading of *The Sun Also Rises* not as an act of settlement or final explanation; however, having concerned ourselves almost exclusively with the way Hemingway's art was formed and how it seems to work in special contexts, it will be salutary to see if we can apply some of these general principles to what is unanimously agreed to be one of his superior artistic productions.

The difficulties of interpreting *The Sun Also Rises* in a clear and relatively certain manner stem in the main from two factors: the use of a particularly opaque first-person narrator; and the fact of Jake's wound which has rendered him impotent, while leaving him normally responsive to sexual desire. The first factor results in the bewilderment a reader will have in trying to locate the norms of "truth" in the novel; that is, since the entire novel is related directly by Jake Barnes, the reader can never be sure how reliable Jake's observations and judgments are. He does not know to what extent he must look at Jake ironically and to what extent sympathetically. And Hemingway has artfully (or accidentally) failed to provide the reader with obvious hints or standards of measurement within the novel which will aid the reader in directing his point of view. Thus, if the reader accepts Jake's story as completely authoritative, he must accept as well Jake's friends and their empty reboundings from one Parisian cabaret to another, from France to Spain and back to France again. If he decides, on top of that, that Jake is Hemingway's sympathetic spokesman, he can only conclude that the "tragedy" of the novel is inherent in Jake's inability to join in the fun. Decisions that Jake is an unreliable narrator, or that he is meant to be unsympathetic will lead to equally absurd readings in an opposite direction. Obviously he must be *mostly* reliable and *mostly* sympathetic. We will try to thread the precarious line of his maneuverings.

The fact of the wound separates Jake from the action in a way that makes this novel very different from all Hemingway's longer fictions. Jake's impotency deprives him of a typical Hemingway love-relationship, and because of the *milieu* in which the novel is placed, it forces him to be a spectator rather than a participator in the events of the novel. He can react intensely, but his actions will necessarily be passive; they will be struggles to "hold on" and to accept rather than to shape circumstances by the force of his direct will. Thus the novel is composed largely of "what happens" to Jake and how he copes with these happenings over which he is denied any control. In a sense this places him in a constant psychological situation of having to accept the absurd meaninglessness of his fate and somehow wrest some meaning from it. Hemingway makes special reference to his "biblical name," Jacob. This may suggest that like his namesake, Jake must wrestle until daybreak with an angel that is a demon; but, unlike his namesake, the "blessing" that will reward his powers to endure will merely ensure the prolongation of the struggle.

Jake's most elaborate statement of his code occurs during the fiesta at Pamplona. It is also close enough to the Hemingway code that we have seen in operation to stand as the value center of the novel:

> I thought I had paid for everything. Not like the woman pays and pays and pays. No idea of retribution or punishment. Just exchange of values. You gave up something and got something else. Or you worked for something. You paid some way for everything that was any good. I paid my way into enough things that I liked, so that I had a good time. Either you paid by learning about them, or by experience, or by taking chances, or by money. Enjoying living was learning to get your money's worth and knowing when you had it. You could get your money's worth. The world was a good place to buy in. It seemed like a fine philosophy. In five years, I thought, it will seem just as silly as all the other fine philosophies I've had.
>
> Perhaps that wasn't true though. Perhaps as you went along you did learn something. I did not care what it was all about. All I wanted to know was how to live in it. Maybe if you found out how to live in it you learned from that what it was all about.

If we can accept this statement as being true for Jake, it should follow that the novel will be a recording of Jake's painful lessons in learning how to live in the world while getting his money's worth of enjoyment for the price that is exacted from him. We can then, at least as a point of departure, examine the story as an "epistemological" novel.

From this standpoint the novel contains one tutor, Count Mippipopolous, and one anti-tutor, Robert Cohn. The Count has presumably paid in full for his ability to enjoy his champagne, his chauffeur, and his expensive tastes in women (he offers Brett $10,000 to go to Biarritz with him). His somewhat incongruous arrow wounds testify to the fact that "he has been there" and has learned how to extract values from his experience. His role as model is pointed to in an early three-way conversation with Brett and Jake:

> "I told you he was one of us. Didn't I?" Brett turned to me. "I love you, count. You're a darling."
> "You make me very happy, my dear. But it isn't true."
> "Don't be an ass."
> "You see, Mr. Barnes, it is because I have lived very much that now I can enjoy everything so well. Don't you find it like that?"
> "Yes. Absolutely."
> "I know," said the count. "That is the secret. You must get to know the values."
> "Doesn't anything ever happen to your values?" Brett asked.
> "No. Not any more."
> "Never fall in love?"
> "Always," said the count. "I am always in love."
> "What does that do to your values?"
> "That, too, has got a place in my values."
> "You haven't any values. You're dead, that's all."
> "No, my dear. You're not right. I'm not dead at all."

The Count is more or less in the position of the Major's ideal man ("In Another Country") who has found things that he cannot lose. He has stripped his stockpile of illusions to the barest minimum, transferring the capitalistic ethic of exchange values to the sphere of the emotions. But, as he corrects Brett, he is not "dead," nor are his emotional transactions mutely mechanical or sterile. His moral position can be compared to that of the gambler who is willing to bet beyond the law of percentages; who will extend and back his play with a calculated risk of losing because part of the gusto of living (to "enjoy everything so well") depends on the exhilaration of exposure. The "stuffed-animal" conversation between Bill Gorton and Jake which occurs shortly after the above scene reinforces this distinction. Bill drunkenly tries to persuade Jake to buy a stuffed dog:

> "Mean everything in the world to you after you bought it. Simple exchange of values. You give them money. They give you a stuffed dog."
> "We'll get one on the way back."
> "All right. Have it your own way. Road to hell paved with unbought stuffed dogs. Not my fault."

And several pages later Jake introduces Bill as a "taxidermist." "That was in another country," Bill said. "And besides all the animals were dead."

Beneath the current of wisecracking (and the dialogue here, as well as in the Burguete scenes, shows Hemingway's superb mastery of sophisticated stage talk), the Count's philosophy is contrasted and given higher valuation. A graded hierarchy of exchange value is implicitly established; the Count insists on a fair exchange; he will pay, but he wants his animals to be "live" and not stuffed. And he has trained himself to be an unillusioned connoisseur in distinguishing between life and its varied imitations. Bill's adaptation of the code is on a lower level of enjoyment. The "road to hell is paved with unbought stuffed dogs." He has no illusions about what he is paying for; he knows that all the animals are dead, but he is willing to forgo the supreme risk of paying for "life," by pursuing the pleasures that he can momentarily extract in the meaningless excitement of his "stuffed animals." His drunken trip to Vienna and his general behavior in Paris are a prelude to Frederick Henry's furlough in *A Farewell to Arms*, because Bill's commitment to enjoyment does not include a real risk of himself. And his position is representative of most of the sophisticated carousers who find an adequate symbol for their desires in the San Fermin fiesta in Pamplona.

But there is also a lower level of gradation in the "exchange-value" metaphor. The road to hell can be traveled swiftly by those who buy stuffed animals, since this is a considered purchase of ultimate emptiness and non-meaning. But that same road, as Hemingway makes clear in his insertion of the scenes with Woolsey and Krum—or with the Dayton, Ohio, pilgrims—is also paved with *unbought* stuffed animals. To deny oneself the ephemeral pleasures, even though they are without meaning, without having a more substantial value to embrace is an even emptier behavior.

There are degrees of *rigor mortis* in the death-in-life as we see in the following expertly understated conversation:

> "Playing any tennis?" Woolsey asked.
> "Well, no," said Krum. "I can't say I've played any this year. I've tried to get away, but Sundays it's always rained, and the courts are so damned crowded."
> "The Englishmen all have Saturday off," Woolsey said.
> "Lucky beggars," said Krum. "Well, I'll tell you. Some day I'm not going to be working for an agency. Then I'll have plenty of time to get out in the country."
> "That's the thing to do. Live out in the country and have a little car."

To use the terminology that we have hitherto employed, the Woolseys and the Krums are unknowing tourists in life, paying exorbitant prices for nothing; the Bill Gortons are professional tourists who pay without illusions for the nothingness that they are willing to settle for; and the Count is the non-tourist professional who is determined to get his money's worth at the expense of exposing himself in the imposition of meaning on his emotional purchases.

This hierarchy of values is highlighted by the presence of the anti-tutor, Robert Cohn, who has the unfortunate burden of being "the horrible example" of the novel. He is Jake Barnes's "double," as it were; he is the secret sharer who suffers cruel and comical ignominy in order to demonstrate to Jake the dangers inherent in "letting go" and falling into the pit of self-deception. First we should note the similarities between Jake and "his tennis friend." They are both writers, they both fall in love with Brett Ashley, they are both superior to the meaningless swirl of drinking, promiscuity, and aimless pleasure seeking which surrounds them. Unlike the others they realize that there are stakes in the game that life has forced them to play; they are, in their different ways, equally concerned to impose meanings on their purchases and receive their money's worth. But Cohn, unlike the Count, has never "been there"; and because of the faults of his temperament, Cohn never will be there. His arrow wounds are both superficial and self-inflicted; he refuses to pay the price of self-knowledge because he has become an expert in the illusion-creating art of self-deception.

Cohn's role of "double" is cast early in the novel when he tells Jake that he can't stand to think that his life is ebbing away and he is "not really living it."

"Listen, Jake," he leaned forward on the bar. "Don't you ever get the feeling that all your life is going by and you're not taking advantage of it? Do you realize you've lived nearly half the time you have to live already?"

"Yes, every once in a while."

"Do you know that in about thirty-five years more we'll be dead?"

"What the hell, Robert," I said. "What the hell."

"I'm serious."

"It's one thing I don't worry about," I said.

"You ought to."

When Cohn proposes a trip to South America, Jake tells him that "going to another country doesn't make any difference. . . . You can't get away from yourself by moving from one place to another. There's nothing to that." Cohn's adamant refusal to look nakedly at himself leaves him incapable of seeing anything external to himself with clarity. He demands that his experiences be measurable in terms of absolutes—his affair with Frances, his writing, his love for Brett; and, when his fortunes become compounded in misery, he demands absolution for his sins of misjudgment. In a remarkable scene of reverse tutorial confrontation, he begs Jake for forgiveness for his actions at Pamplona. If we remember the previously quoted conversation between Robert Jordan and Anselmo on forgiveness, it will show us how far outside the code Cohn stands:

> He was crying without any noise.
> "I just couldn't stand it about Brett. I've been through hell, Jake. It's been simply hell. When I met her down here Brett treated me as though I were a perfect stranger. I just couldn't stand it. We lived together at San Sebastian. I suppose you know it. I can't stand it any more."
> "I guess it isn't any use," he said. "I guess it isn't any damn use."
> "What?"
> "Everything. Please say you forgive me Jake."
> "Sure," I said. "It's all right."
> "I felt so terribly. I've been through such hell, Jake. Now everything's gone. Everything."

Robert Cohn capitulates unconditionally to the rule of *nada* through his refusal to give up his illusions; and although his intentions are far more admirable than that of the others who give in to the empty enjoyment of nothingness, his fate is to be the most despicable character that Hemingway ever created; he is similar to but worse than Richard Gordon in *To Have and Have Not*.

The delicate web of differing values is subtly suggested in the death of Vincente Girones, the twenty-eight-year-old farmer from Tafalla who has come every year to the fiesta at Pamplona to join in the *encierro*, the running of the bulls through the streets to the bull ring. Jake sees him tossed and gored as the bulls and the crowd of merrymakers sweep over and past him to the ring. When Jake returns to the café, he reports the event to the waiter:

> The waiter nodded his head and swept the crumbs from the table with his cloth.
> "Badly cogida," he said. "All for sport. All for pleasure. . . . A big horn wound. All for fun. Just for fun. What do you think of that?"
> "I don't know."
> "That's it. All for fun. Fun, for understand."
> "You're not an aficionado?"
> "Me? What are bulls? Animals. Brute animals. . . . You hear? Muerte. Dead. He's dead. With a horn through him. All for morning fun. Es muy flamenco."
> "It's bad."
> "Not for me," the waiter said. "No fun in that for me."

Later Jake reports that the bull which gored Girones was killed by Pedro Romero and its ear was given to Brett, who left it with her cigarette butts in the bedside table of her hotel room. And later, after Bill has reported to Jake a full account of Cohn's activities on the night before, Jake tells him that a man had been killed in the runway outside the ring. " 'Was there?' said Bill."

This episode, deceptively trivial in its presentation, is a measure of Hemingway's control over the dramatic irony with which the novel is narrated. Girones' death is the single event of absolute human importance in the entire novel. All the infidelities, quarrels, and carousals of the principal characters fade into insubstantiality in comparison with the man who "lay face down in the trampled mud." Even the courage and dexterity with which Romero performs in the ring becomes a theatrical gesturing in contrast to the finality and absurdity of this immutable death. And Bill's incapacity to react humanly to that death is a telling indication of his (and the others') deficiencies in a full knowledge and understanding of the code.

For Girones is a symbol of the fatal and unchangeable stakes that are involved in the game that all the characters are playing. He leaves his wife and two children to run with the bulls, but he must pay with his life for his "fun." Like Robert Cohn, Girones is tossed and gored; it is probable that he dies "full of illusions"; but, in terms of the code, he fails to get his money's worth for his death. Bill and the others have become practised in ignoring the prices they will have to pay for their "fun" also. The consequences of their variety of self-deceit is a constant death-in-life because they have chosen to accept the rule of "nothingness," becoming servitors to its reign in the frenzy of their acceptance. Girones' death is the physical fact of their living deaths, and their inability to respond to it establishes clearly to what extent they have died.

Here we should perhaps deal with Brett's famous act of self-abnegation, her decision to send Romero away because she will not be "one of these bitches that ruins children." In terms of the dramatic context of the novel, her action is meant to be taken seriously; and it leads directly to the definition of moraltiy which Hemingway later voiced in his own person in *Death in the Afternoon:*

> "You know I feel rather damned good, Jake."
> "You should."
> "You know it makes one feel rather good deciding not to be a bitch."
> "Yes."
> "It's sort of what we have instead of God."
> "Some people have God," I said. "Quite a lot."
> "He never worked very well with me."

It is too easily possible, I believe, to accept this scene at face value and to forget that it is filtered through Jake's narration and that its fictional meaning will depend on the values with which Jake colors it. In our earlier discussion of the code, we noticed that Hemingway demanded certain basic prerequisites from his characters before he would allow their emotional reactions to be considered worthy gauges of morality. They would have to have learned the hard way what the stakes in the game involved, and they would have to be willing to shed their illusions in their fight to force meaning out of life. It is difficult to feel that Brett meets these qualifications. She has had an unenviable time with her previous husband; she claims to be in love with Jake; she is a near-alcoholic and a near-nymphomaniac. At the end of the novel she casts her lot—whether permanent or temporary it is impossible to determine—with Mike who has made a career out of irresponsibility. What we know of Brett is what Jake chooses to divulge, and his position makes him a considerably biased observer.

He tells himself at one point that she thinks she is in love with him because he is something that she cannot have. It is certainly true that her love develops after Jake's incapacitating wound. She is ready to despise Robert Cohn because he could not believe that their stay in San Sebastiian "didn't mean anything." She also has a good deal of contempt for Cohn because he allows his "suffering" to show. And yet, if we are to accept her sacrifice of Romero as an act of positive morality and in terms of her own stated code, we must judge her as severely as she judges Cohn. She cannot believe that her affair with Romero "didn't mean anything," and she makes no attempt to conceal her suffering. Jake's response to her speech on morality ("Some people have God.") may indicate his detachment from her use of the "we" in the previous sentence ("It's sort of what we have instead of God."). And similarly, the marvellously ambiguous ending of the novel would indicate Jake's holding himself apart from the illusions which Brett has voiced:

> "Oh, Jake," Brett said, "we could have had such a damned good time together."
> Ahead was a mounted policeman in khaki directing traffic. He raised his baton. The car slowed suddenly pressing Brett against me.
> "Yes," I said. "Isn't it pretty to think so?"

But Jake has learned—in part from Count Mippipopolous—that illusions (sure beliefs projected into the future) are the first things one must discard if one wants to learn how to live life. In order to see this ambiguity more clearly, we must reinvestigate Jake's role as narrator.

When we meet Jake at the beginning of the novel he is in the process of recovering from his wound and of attempting to learn how to live with it. His days are easily occupied with the seemingly simple tasks of newspaper correspondent and café habitué; the nights are more difficult for him to stand, since his wound, unlike the Count's, still throbs and gives him pain. He has detached himself completely from his Kansas City background and is relatively uninvolved with any of the Parisian set, although all claim him as a friend. He has three passions only: fishing, bullfighting, and Brett. The first two he is able to indulge in with full enjoyment—getting his money's worth and knowing when he has had it. The third is an impossibility on which he expends an inordinate amount of psychic energy and pain. Brett is something that he can neither afford nor even gamble for. And his meagre pleasures for the price that he pays become less and less. In fact, his relationship to Brett is a pathetic parallel to Vincente Girones' with the San Fermin fiesta. Like Girones, Jake exposes himself to the dangers of being gored and of being trampled "all for fun," except that the "fun" is pain. Brett is his fiesta, as we see in the image of Brett with the white garlic wreath around her neck surrounded by the circle of *riau-riau* dancers. And the lesson that he learns from the sharp juxtaposition of his idyllic pleasures at Burguete and the misery of Pamplona is that he "was through with fiestas for a while." Just as Frederick Henry has to learn that a truly human life demands involvement or "caring-ness," so Jake Barnes must learn to become uninvolved from useless and impossible illusions if he is to remain sane.

This, it seems to me, is the point of his breaking the code of the true *aficionado* that loses him the respect of Montoya. Hemingway tells us that "Aficion means passion. An aficionado is one who is passionate about bullfights." But, as we have seen, Hemingway extends the concept of *aficion* to include the "passion" which the code requires for an honest confrontation of *nada*. And thus Jake falls from the ethics of the code badly in his arranging of the liaison between Brett and Romero. Montoya, who could forgive anything of one who had *aficion*, cannot forgive the *aficionado* who has degraded his passion. In pursuing the vain illusion of Brett, Jake too succumbs to self-deception and self-treachery, since he throws away a self-respect which he does not need to lose. His decision to remain at San Sebastian and the descriptions of his restrained enjoyment in swimming, walking, reading, and eating are reminiscent of his controlled pleasures while fishing in Burguete. His comments on himself, after sending an answer to Brett's telegram, are not just ironic; they are revelatory of the lesson he is learning: "That was it. Send a girl off with one man. Introduce her to another to go off with him. Now go and bring her back. And sign the wire with love. That was it all right." Here, even under the disguise of self-dramatization, he is facing the truth of his actions and preparing himself for his renunciation of the impossible illusion that Brett represents. In this context his description of his arrival in Madrid has strong symbolic overtones of the decision that is on the verge of coalescence: "The Norte station in Madrid is the end of the line. All trains finish there. They don't go on anywhere." Jake too has reached the end of the line with this "vanity" that has sapped his emotional strength.

In the ensuing conversation with Brett, Jake's role is that of the "counterpuncher." His answers to her remarks are restrained and couched in a defensive irony which protects his detachment without exposing him to attack. His appetite at Botin's is keen; and although he feels the need to brace himself with wine, this is more an act of propitiation to the pain of his disseverance from an old self than a capitulation to despair. And in the final ambiguous lines which we have quoted earlier, the detachment is made complete. The policeman directing traffic raises his baton in a wonderfully suggestive gesture, both phallic and symbolic of the new command that Jake has issued to himself; and the car in which he and Brett are riding slows down suddenly. "Yes. Isn't it pretty to think so?" commemorates Jake's separate peace with himself and his new determination to live his life by those passions which are within the scope of his powers and conducive to the possibilities of his self-realization in his pursuit of them.

The structure and the ironic narrative perspective of *The Sun Also Rises* are thus the subtle explicator and shaper of its meanings. Remembering Hemingway's explanation of the three acts of the bullfight, we can find the hint of a parallel in the three-book division into which *The Sun Also Rises* falls. Book One is "the trial of the lances," in which Jake is painfully "pic-ed" by the barbs of his unresignable desire for a free expression of his natural wants; Book Two, the act of the bandilleras at Pamplona, goads him beyond endurance into jealousy and self-betrayal; and Book Three, the final division of death, is the brave administering of *quietus* to that part of his life desire which he must learn to live without if he is to live at all. The mode of narration in which the "lesson" of self-growth is presented obliquely and almost beneath the conscious awareness of the narrator-protagonist creates the problem of interpretation, but it also insures the vitality and ironic tensions within which the novel changes its shape and suggests multiple meanings. Jake is both sympathetic and reliable narrator ultimately, but his emergence as a full-fledged, graduating tyro hero is gained only after he has fallen several times, forced himself to admit his failures to himself, and secured his own forgiveness. As we have seen in our previous discussions of Hemingway's fiction, it is "the irony of the unsaid" that says most clearly and resonantly what the stripped usable values are, and what one has to pay for them.

On this base of interpretation we must now look briefly at a wider range of meanings that may explain the power and popular success of this novel. Surely the "story' we have outlined above is too bleak and spare in itself to have generated the response and wide acclamation that *The Sun Also Rises* has received since its publication. For this novel, more than any other of Hemingway's, has been cherished as a cultural document—a work of art which makes that miraculous conjunction with the spirit of the times so as to seem both distillation and artistic resolution of the prevailing temper of the age out of which it rises. Oscar Cargill points to one obvious source of its cultural apeal in his *Intellectual America:* "*The Sun Also Rises* has no peer among American books that have attempted to take account of the cost of the War upon the morals of the War generation and ... [there are] no better polemics against war than this, which was meant for no polemic at all."

Coming four years after Eliot's *The Waste Land* and three years before Faulkner's *The Sound and the Fury*, *The Sun Also Rises*—like its two peers in American writing of the 1920's— succeeds in merging the unique psychological crisis of its author with the cultural crisis of its time. "After such knowledge what forgiveness?" is perhaps the agonizing question that informs the best writings of the 1920's. World War I had been the catalytic agent in releasing the stark factor of nothingness and absurdity at the very root of traditional values. And the theme which powerfully insinuates itself into the best literary documents of the postwar period is the theme of the emotional paralysis with which sensitivity is overwhelmed at the hideous realization that life makes no sense except in those tenuous designs which enervated man himself imposes upon it. It is within the reverberations of this theme that *The Sun Also Rises* transcends its idiosyncrasies of unrepresentative locale and its restricted range of action to become a compelling and universalized metaphor for its era as well as ours.

The cause and the nature of Jake Barnes's wound force his experiences into a level of symbolic relevance which makes his slow, uncertain struggle to regain a positive stance toward life as much a parable as an "epistemological" romance. It is "the dirty war" that has crippled him, just as it has indirectly crippled the others who fritter and burn in the hells of the *bal musette* and in the pandemonic stampede of the *encierro*. Without the war as a causative background these would be merely empty and sick people who drain their lives away into the receding blue notes of a jazz orchestra; but the war was a fact, and it was one which stripped the veil of pious sanctimony and patriotic veneer from the spurious moralities and ethics of traditional American "boosterism" in religion, philosophy, and politics. The expatriates of *The Sun Also Rises* are sensitive recorders of the shock which they have suffered and of the distance that has been created between themselves and those back in America who "lived in it [*nada*] and never felt it."

As characters who are truly "ex-patriated," they live in another country where all the stuffed values of the past in which they were trained are dead: " 'You're an expatriate. You've lost touch with the soil. You get precious. Fake European standards have ruined you. You drink yourself to death. You become obsessed by sex. You spend all your time talking, not working. You're an expatriate, see? You hang around cafés.' "

And while it is true, as we have seen in our analysis of the hierarchy of exchange value in *The Sun Also Rises*, that the war and the consequent moral vacuum were mere excuses, for many of these "expatriates," for a life of empty sensationalism with the flimsy justification of arrogance and revolt, yet it is also true that for some—and especially Jake—the stock market of morality has crashed and the bottom has fallen out of an instinctive *rationale* for life.

For *The Sun Also Rises* is a good deal more than a polemic against war. It does show the battle casualties, and it does demonstrate that others than those in the direct line of fire were grievously crippled by flying shell fragments. But far beyond this, and much more important, it is a reassertion of the basic truth of American culture (integral to that culture, if too frequently buried under concealing platitudes) that individual man is the puny maker of his meanings in life. If he does not impose them out of an integrity to the unvarnished truths of his own experience, then they will not exist at all—and unmeaning will flood into the vacuum of his irresolution. The "wilderness" of eighteenth-century American literature and the unfathomable "frontier" of the nineteenth century fuse and echo hollowly in the *nada* of the twentieth century, but the challenge is the same and the possible creative responses to that challenge are just as limited in number. It was probably a fortuitous accident that Hemingway's personal wound and relationship of estrangement from the Booth Tarkington *mores* of Oak Park should result in the compelling symbolism of *The Sun Also Rises*, but such are the graces of literary history.

Jake Barnes's wound paralyzes him at the roots of his being. He has the desire to act, coupled with a hypersensitive capacity to react; but he cannot make appropriate responses because his powers of creativity—his powers of self-generation—have atrophied as the symbolic result of his wound. He is not unlike Eliot's Gerontion or his Fisher-King who sit in despair, praying for the miracle of rain. Nor is he wholly unlike Faulkner's Quentin Compson whose similar despair and similar incapacity result from his inability to rid himself of a burdensome, life-denying past. But on a symbolic level, Jake's struggle is not ineffectual; and, it is in profound harmony with earlier American literary struggles with despair before the confrontation of nothingness. He creates his own miracle of rain, irrigating his dead lands out of the fructifying love of life to which his passion for nature (Burguete) and his admiration for human heroism (the bullfights) testify. And he is able to force himself to a new beginning, eradicating the determinism of his past —his wound, his self-treachery and degeneration with Brett— through self-forgiveness and faith in his own human resources which, like the earth, "abideth forever" in the granite veins of humanity.

Thus, *The Sun Also Rises* combines in one radical metaphor the two antithetical halves of the broad humanistic tradition that goes back to Ecclesiastes. It documents in full, unsparing detail the meaningless ant lives of petty, ephemeral humanity making its small noise of pleasure and sacrifice in the boundless and unheeding auditorium of eternity: "Vanity of vanities, saith the Preacher, vanity of vanities; all is vanity. What profit hath a man of all his labour which he taketh under the sun? One generation passeth away, and another generation cometh; but the earth abideth forever. The sun also ariseth, and the sun goeth down, and hasteth to his place where he arose."

And yet, without compromising this merciless vision of the compounded vanities by which even the best of the human race lives, Hemingway erects a tenuous but believable bridge across the shadow of nothingness in Jake Barnes's determined wrestle for meaning. The title of the novel pays its just obeisance to the cynical wisdom of the ancient Hebraic Preacher of Ecclesiastes; but in its exhortatory and unillusioned chronicling of man's heroic powers to create values out of himself, it also echoes Emerson's similar considered faith that "The sun shines to-day also."

Mark Spilka

The Death of Love in
The Sun Also Rises

> She turns and looks a moment in the glass,
> Hardly aware of her departed lover;
> Her brain allows one half-formed thought to pass;
> "Well now that's done: and I'm glad it's over."
> When lovely woman stoops to folly and
> Paces about her room again, alone,
> She smooths her hair with automatic hand,
> And puts a record on the gramophone.
>
> T. S. Eliot, *The Waste Land*

One of the most persistent themes of the twenties was the death of love in World War I. All the major writers recorded it, often in piecemeal fashion, as part of the larger postwar scene; but only Hemingway seems to have caught it whole and delivered it in lasting fictional form. His intellectual grasp of the theme might account for this. Where D. H. Lawrence settles for the shock of war on the Phallic Consciousness, or where Eliot presents assorted glimpses of sterility, Hemingway seems to design an extensive

From *Twelve Original Essays on Great American Novels,* ed., Charles Shapiro (Detroit, Mich.: Wayne State University Press, 1958), 238-256. Copyright 1958 by the Wayne State University Press. Reprinted by permission of the publishers.

parable. Thus, in *The Sun Also Rises*, his protagonists are deliberately shaped as allegorical figures: Jake Barnes and Brett Ashley are two lovers desexed by the war; Robert Cohn is the false knight who challenges their despair; while Romero, the stalwart bullfighter, personifies the good life which will survive their failure. Of course, these characters are not abstractions in the text; they are realized through the most concrete style in American fiction; and their larger meaning is implied only by their response to immediate situations. But the implications are there, the parable is at work in every scene, and its presence lends unity and depth to the whole novel.

Barnes himself is a fine example of this technique. Cut off from love by a shell wound, he seems to suffer from an undeserved misfortune. But as most readers agree, his condition represents a peculiar form of emotional impotence. It does not involve distaste for the flesh, as with Lawrence's crippled veteran, Clifford Chatterley; instead Barnes lacks the power to control love's strength and durability. His sexual wound, the result of an unpreventable "accident" in the war, points to another realm where accidents can always happen and where Barnes is equally powerless to prevent them. In Book II of the novel he makes this same comparison while describing one of the dinners at Pamplona: "It was like certain dinners I remember from the war. There was much wine, an ignored tension, and a feeling of things coming that you could not prevent happening." This fear of emotional consequences is the key to Barnes's condition. Like so many Hemingway heroes, he has no way to handle subjective complications, and his wound is a token of this kind of impotence.

It serves the same purpose for the expatriate crowd in Paris. In some figurative manner these artists, writers, and derelicts have all been rendered impotent by the war. Thus, as Barnes presents them, they pass before us like a parade of sexual cripples, and we are able to measure them against his own forbearance in the face of a common problem. Whoever bears his sickness well is akin to Barnes; whoever adopts false postures, or willfully hurts others, falls short of his example. This is the organizing principle in Book I, this alignment of characters by their stoic qualities. But, stoic or not, they are all incapable of love, and in their sober moments they seem to know it.

For this reason they feel especially upset whenever Robert Cohn appears. Cohn still upholds a romantic view of life, and since he affirms it with stubborn persistence, he acts like a goad upon his wiser contemporaries. As the narrator, Barnes must account for the challenge he presents them and the decisive turn it takes in later chapters. Accordingly, he begins the book with a review of Cohn's boxing career at Princeton. Though he has no taste for it, college boxing means a lot to Cohn. For one thing, it helps to compensate for anti-Semitic treatment from his classmates. More subtly, it turns him into an armed romantic, a man who can damage others in defense of his own beliefs. He also loves the pose of manhood which it affords him and seems strangely pleased when his nose is flattened in the ring. Soon other tokens of virility delight him, and he often confuses them with actual manliness. He likes the idea of a mistress more than he likes his actual mistress; or he likes the authority of editing and the prestige of writing, though he is a bad editor and a poor novelist. In other words, he always looks for internal strength in outward signs and sources. On leaving Princeton, he marries "on the rebound from the rotten time . . . in college." But in five years the marriage falls through, and he rebounds again to his present mistress, the forceful Frances Clyne. Then, to escape her dominance and his own disquiet, he begins to look for romance in far-off countries. As with most of his views, the source of this idea is an exotic book:

> He had been reading W. H. Hudson. That sounds like an innocent occupation, but Cohn had read and reread "The Purple Land." "The Purple Land" is a very sinister book if read too late in life. It recounts splendid imaginary amorous adventures of a perfect English gentleman in an intensely romantic land, the scenery of which is very well described. For a man to take it at thirty-four as a guidebook to what life holds is about as safe as it would be for a man of the same age to enter Wall Street direct from a French convent, equipped with a complete set of the more practical Alger books. Cohn, I believe, took every word of "The Purple Land" as literally as though it had been an R. G. Dun report.

Cohn's romanticism explains his key position in the parable. He is the last chivalric hero, the last defender of an outworn faith, and his function is to illustrate its present folly—to show us, through the absurdity of his behavior, that romantic love is dead, that one of the great guiding codes of the past no longer operates. "You're getting damned romantic," says Brett to Jake at one point in the novel. "No, bored," he replies, because for this generation boredom has become more plausible than love. As a foil to his contemporaries, Cohn helps to reveal why this is so.

Of course, there is much that is traditional in the satire on Cohn. Like the many victims of romantic literature, from Don Quixote to Tom Sawyer, he lives by what he reads and neglects reality at his own and others' peril. But Barnes and his friends have no alternative to Cohn's beliefs. There is nothing here, for example, like the neat balance between sense and sensibility in Jane Austen's world. Granted that Barnes is sensible enough, that he sees life clearly and that we are meant to contrast his private grief with Cohn's public suffering, his self-restraint with Cohn's deliberate self-exposure. Yet, emasculation aside, Barnes has no way to measure or control the state of love; and though he recognizes this with his mind and tries to act accordingly, he seems no different from Cohn in his deepest feelings. When he is alone with Brett, he wants to live with her in the country, to go with her to San Sebastian, to go up to her room, to keep her in his own room, or to keep on kissing her—though he can never really act upon such sentiments. Nor are they merely the yearnings of a tragically impotent man, for eventually they will lead Barnes to betray his own principles and to abandon self-respect, all for the sake of Lady Ashley. No, at best he is a restrained romantic, a man who carries himself well in the face of love's impossibilities, but who seems to share with Cohn a common (if hidden) weakness.

The sexual parade continues through the early chapters. Besides Cohn and his possessive mistress, there is the prostitute Georgette, whom Barnes picks up one day "because of a vague sentimental idea that it would be nice to eat with someone." Barnes introduces her to his friends as his fiancée, and as his private joke affirms, the two have much in common. Georgette is sick and sterile, having reduced love to a simple monetary exchange; but, like Barnes, she manages to be frank and forthright and to keep an even keel among the drifters of Paris. Together they form a pair of honest cripples, in contrast with the various pretenders whom they meet along the Left Bank. Among the latter are Cohn and Frances Clyne, the writer Braddocks and his wife, and Robert Prentiss, a rising young novelist who seems to verbalize their phoniness: "Oh, how charmingly you get angry," he tells Barnes. "I wish I had that faculty." Barnes's honest anger has been aroused by the appearance of a band of homosexuals, accompanied by Brett Ashley. When one of the band spies Georgette, he decides to dance with her; then one by one the rest follow suit, in deliberate parody of normal love. Brett herself provides a key to the dizzy sexual medley. With a man's felt hat on her boyish bob, and with her familiar reference to men as fellow "chaps," she completes the distortion of sexual roles which seems to characterize the period. For the war, which has unmanned Barnes and his contemporaries, has turned Brett into the freewheeling equal of any man. It has taken her first sweetheart's life through dysentery and has sent her present husband home in a dangerous state of shock. For Brett these blows are the equivalent of Jake's emasculation; they seem to release her from her womanly nature and expose her to the male prerogatives of drink and promiscuity. Once she claims these rights as her own, she becomes an early but more honest version of Catherine Barkley, the English nurse in Hemingway's next important novel, *A Farewell to Arms*. Like Catherine, Brett has been a nurse on the Italian front and has lost a sweetheart in the war; but for her there is no saving interlude of love with a wounded patient, no rigged and timely escape through death in childbirth. Instead she survives the colossal violence, the disruption of her personal life, and the exposure to mass promiscuity, to confront a moral and emotional vacuum among her postwar lovers. With this evidence of male default all around her, she steps off the romantic pedestal, moves freely through the bars of Paris, and stands confidently there beside her newfound equals. Ironically, her most recent conquest, Robert Cohn, fails to see the bearing of such changes on romantic love. He still believes that Brett is womanly and therefore deeply serious about intimate matters. After their first meeting, he describes her as "absolutely fine and straight" and nearly strikes Barnes for thinking otherwise; and a bit later, after their brief affair in the country, he remains unconvinced "that it didn't mean anything." But when men no longer command respect, and women replace their natural warmth with masculine freedom and mobility, there can be no serious love.

Brett does have some respect for Barnes, even a little tenderness, though her actions scarcely show abiding love. At best she can affirm his worth and share his standards and perceptions. When in public, she knows how to keep her essential misery to herself; when alone with Barnes, she will express her feelings, admit her faults, and even display good judgment. Thus her friend Count Mippipopolous is introduced to Barnes as "one of us." The count qualifies by virtue of his war wounds, his invariable calmness, and his curious system of values. He appreciates good food, good wine, and a quiet place in which to enjoy them. Love also has a place in his system, but since he is "always in love," the place seems rather shaky. Like Jake and Brett and perhaps Georgette, he simply bears himself well among the postwar ruins.

The count completes the list of cripples who appear in Book I. In a broader sense, they are all disaffiliates, all men and women who have cut themselves off from conventional society and who have made Paris their permanent playground. Jake Barnes has introduced them, and we have been able to test them against his stoic attitudes toward life in a moral wasteland. Yet such life is finally unbearable, as we have also seen whenever Jake and Brett are alone together, or whenever Jake is alone with his thoughts. He needs a healthier code to live by, and for this reason the movement in Book II is away from Paris to the trout stream at Burguete and the bull ring at Pamplona. Here a more vital testing process occurs, and with the appearance of Bill Gorton we get our first inkling of its nature.

Gorton is a successful writer who shares with Barnes a love for boxing and other sports. In Vienna he has helped to rescue a splendid Negro boxer from an angry and intolerant crowd. The incident has spoiled Vienna for him, and, as his reaction suggests, the sports world will provide the terms of moral judgment from this point onward in the novel. Or, more accurately, Jake Barnes's feelings about sports will shape the rest of the novel. For, with Hemingway, the great outdoors, is chiefly a state of mind, a projection of moral and emotional attitudes onto physical arenas, so that a clear account of surface action will reproduce these attitudes in the reader. In "Big Two-Hearted River," for example, he describes Nick Adams' fishing and camping activities along a trout stream in Michigan. His descriptions run to considerable length, and they are all carefully detailed, almost as if they were meant for a fishing manual. Yet the details themselves have strong emotional connotations for Nick Adams. He thinks of his camp as "the good place," the place where none of his previous troubles can touch him. He has left society behind him, and, as the story begins, there is even a burnt town at his back, to signify his disaffiliation. He has also walked miles to reach an arbitrary camp site, and this is one of the ways in which he sets his own conditions for happiness and then lives up to them. He finds extraordinary pleasure, moreover, in the techniques of making coffee and pitching camp, or in his responses to fishing and eating. In fact, his sensations have become so valuable that he doesn't want to rush them: they bring health, pleasure, beauty, and a sense of order which is sorely missing in his civilized experience; they are part of a healing process, a private and imaginative means of wiping out the damages of civilized life. When this process is described with elaborate attention to surface detail, the effect on the reader is decidedly subjective.

The same holds true, of course, for the fishing trip in *The Sun Also Rises*. As Barnes and Gorton approach "the good place," each item in the landscape is singled out and given its own importance. Later the techniques of fishing are treated with the same reverence for detail. For like Nick Adams, these men have left the wasteland for the green plains of health; they have traveled miles, by train and on foot, to reach a particular trout stream. The fishing there is good, the talk free and easy, and even Barnes is able to sleep well after lunch, though he is usually an insomniac. The meal itself is handled like a mock religious ceremony: "Let us rejoice in our blessings," says Gorton. "Let us utilize the fowls of the air. Let us utilize the produce of the vine. Will you utilize a little, brother?" A few days later, when they visit the old monastery at Roncesvalles, this combination of fishing, drinking, and male camaraderie is given an edge over religion itself. With their English friend, Harris, they honor the monastery as a remarkable place, but decide that "it isn't the same as fishing"; then all agree to "utilize" a little pub across the way. At the trout stream, moreover, romantic love is given the same comparative treatment and seems sadly foolish before the immediate joys of fishing:

> It was a little past noon and there was not much shade, but I sat against the trunk of two of the trees that grew together, and read. The book was something by A. E. W. Mason, and I was reading a wonderful story about a man who had been frozen in the Alps and then fallen into a glacier and disappeared, and his bride was going to wait twenty-four years exactly for his body to come out on the moraine, while her true love waited too, and they were still waiting when Bill came up [with four trout in his bag]. . . . His face was sweaty and happy.

As these comparisons show, the fishing trip has been invested with unique importance. By sticking closely to the surface action, Barnes has evoked the deeper attitudes which underlie it and which make it a therapeutic process for him. He describes himself now as a "rotten Catholic" and speaks briefly of his thwarted love for Brett; but with religion defunct and love no longer possible, he can at least find happiness through private and imaginative means. Thus he now constructs a more positive code to follow: as with Nick Adams, it brings him health, pleasure, beauty and order, and helps to wipe out the damage of his troubled life in Paris.

Yet somehow the code lacks depth and substance. To gain these advantages, Barnes must move to Pamplona, which stands roughly to Burguete as the swamp in "Big Two-Hearted River" stands to the trout stream. In the latter story, Nick Adams prefers the clear portion of the river to its second and more congested heart:

> In the swamp the banks were bare, the big cedars came together overhead, the sun did not come through, except in patches; in the fast deep water, in the half light, the fishing would be tragic. In the swamp fishing was a tragic adventure. Nick did not want it. . . . There were plenty of days coming when he could fish the swamp.

The fishing is tragic here because it involves the risk of death. Nick is not yet ready for that challenge, but plainly it will test his manhood when he comes to face it. In *The Sun Also Rises* Barnes makes no such demands upon himself; but he is strongly attracted to the young bullfighter, Pedro Romero, whose courage before death lends moral weight to the sportsman's code.[1]

So Pamplona is an extension of Burguete for Barnes: gayer and more festive on the surface, but essentially more serious. The spoilers from Paris have arrived, but (Cohn excepted) they are soon swept up by the fiesta: their mood is jubilant, they are surrounded by dancers, and they sing, drink, and shout with the peasant crowd. Barnes himself is among fellow *aficionados;* he gains "real emotion" from the bullfights and feels truly elated afterwards. Even his friends seem like "such nice people," though he begins to feel uneasy when an argument breaks out between them. The tension is created by Brett's fiancé, Mike Campbell, who is aware of her numerous infidelities and who seems to accept them

---

[1] Hemingway's preoccupation with death has been explained in various ways: by his desire to write about simple, fundamental things; by his "sadomasochism"; or, more fairly and accurately, by his need to efface an actual war wound, or to supplant the ugly, senseless violence of war with ordered, graceful violence. Yet chiefly the risk of death lends moral seriousness to a private code which lacks it. The risk is arbitrary; when a man elects to meet it, his beliefs take on subjective weight and he is able to give meaning to his private life. In this sense, he moves forever on a kind of imaginative frontier, where the opposition is always Nature, in some token form, where the stakes are always manliness and self-respect, and where death invests the scene with tragic implications. In *The Sun Also Rises,* Romero lives on such a frontier, and for Barnes and his friends he provides an example of just these values.

with amoral tolerance. Actually he resents them, so that Cohn (the perennial Jewish scapegoat) provides him with a convenient outlet for his feelings. He begins to bait him for following Brett around like a sick steer.

Mike's description is accurate enough. Cohn is always willing to suffer in public and to absorb insults for the sake of true love. On the other hand, he is also "ready to do battle for his lady," and when the chance finally comes, he knocks his rivals down like a genuine knight-errant. With Jake and Mike he has no trouble, but when he charges into Pedro's room to rescue Brett, the results are disastrous: Brett tells him off, the bullfighter refuses to stay knocked down, and no one will shake hands with him at the end, in accord with prep-school custom. When Brett remains with Pedro, Cohn retires to his room, alone and friendless.

This last encounter is the high point of the parable, for in the Code Hero, the Romantic Hero has finally met his match. As the clash between them shows, there is a difference between physical and moral victory, between chivalric stubbornness and real self-respect. Thus Pedro fights to repair an affront to his dignity; though he is badly beaten, his spirit is untouched by his opponent, whereas Cohn's spirit is completely smashed. From the beginning Cohn has based his manhood on skill at boxing, or upon a woman's love, never upon internal strength; but now, when neither skill nor love supports him, he has bludgeoned his way to his own emptiness. Compare his conduct with Romero's, on the following day, as the younger man performs for Brett in the bull ring:

> Everything of which he could control the locality he did in front of her all that afternoon. Never once did he look up. . . . Because he did not look up to ask if it pleased he did it all for himself inside, and it strengthened him, and yet he did it for her, too. But he did not do it for her at any loss to himself. He gained by it all through the afternoon.

Thus, where Cohn expends and degrades himself for his beloved, Romero pays tribute without self-loss. His manhood is a thing independent of women, and for this reason he holds special attractions for Jake Barnes.

By now it seems apparent that Cohn and Pedro are extremes for which Barnes is the unhappy medium. His resemblance to Pedro is clear enough: they share the same code, they both believe that a man's dignity depends on his own resources. His resemblance to Cohn is more subtle, but at this stage of the book it becomes grossly evident. Appropriately enough, the exposure comes through the knockout blow from Cohn, which dredges up a strange prewar experience:

> Walking across the square to the hotel everything looked new and changed. . . . I felt as I felt once coming home from an out-of-town football game. I was carrying a suitcase with my football things in it, and I walked up the street from the station in the town I had lived in all my life and it was all new. They were raking the lawns and burning leaves in the road, and I stopped for a long time and watched. It was all strange. Then I went on, and my feet seemed to be a long way off, and everything seemed to come from a long way off, and I could hear my feet walking a great distance away. I had been kicked in the head early in the game. It was like that crossing the square. It was like that going up the stairs in the hotel. Going up the stairs took a long time, and I had the feeling that I was carrying my suitcase.

Barnes seems to have regressed here to his youthful football days. As he moves on up the stairs to see Cohn, who has been asking for him, he still carries his "phantom suitcase" with him; and when he enters Cohn's room, he even sets it down. Cohn himself has just returned from the fight with Romero: "There he was, face down on the bed, crying. He had on a white polo shirt, the kind he'd worn at Princeton." In other words, Cohn has also regressed to his abject college days: they are both emotional adolescents, about the same age as the nineteen-year-old Romero, who is the only real man among them. Of course, these facts are not spelled out for us, except through the polo shirt and the phantom suitcase, which remind us (inadvertently) of one of those dream-like fantasies by the Czech genius Franz Kafka, in which trunks and youthful clothes are symbols of arrested development. Yet there has already been some helpful spelling out in Book I, during a curious (and otherwise pointless) exchange between Cohn and another expatriate, the drunkard Harvey Stone. After first calling Cohn a moron, Harvey asks him to say, without thinking about it, what he would rather do if he could do anything he wanted. Cohn is again urged to say what comes into his head first, and soon replies, "I think I'd rather play football again with what I know about handling myself, now." To which Harvey responds: "I misjudged you. . . . You're not a moron. You're only a case of arrested development."

The first thought to enter Cohn's mind here has been suppressed by Barnes for a long time, but in Book II the knockout blow releases it: more than anything else, he too would like to "play football again," to prevent that kick to his head from happening, or that smash to the jaw from Cohn, or that sexual wound which explains either blow. For the truth about Barnes seems obvious now: he has always been an emotional adolescent. Like Nick Adams, he has grown up in a society which has little use for manliness; as an expression of that society, the war has robbed him of his dignity as a man and has thus exposed him to indignities with women. We must understand here that the war, the early football game, and the fight with Cohn have this in common: they all involve ugly, senseless, or impersonal forms of violence, in which a man has little chance to set the terms of his own integrity. Hence for Hemingway they represent the kinds of degradation which can occur at any point in modern society—and the violence at Pamplona is our current sample of such degradation. Indeed, the whole confluence of events now points to the social meaning of Jake's wound, for just as Cohn has reduced him to a dazed adolescent, so has Brett reduced him to a slavish pimp. When she asks for his help in her affair with Pedro, Barnes has no integrity to rely on; he can only serve her as Cohn has served her, like a sick romantic steer. Thus, for love's sake, he will allow her to use him as a go-between, to disgrace him with his friend Montoya, to corrupt Romero, and so strip the whole fiesta of significance. In the next book he will even run to her rescue in Madrid, though by then he can at least recognize his folly and supply his own indictment: "That was it. Send a girl off with one man. Introduce her to another to go off with him. Now go and bring her back. And sign the wire with love. That was it all right." It seems plain, then, that Cohn and Brett have given us a peacetime demonstration, postwar style, of the meaning of Jake's shell wound.

At Pamplona the demonstration continues. Brett strolls through the fiesta with her head high, "as though [it] were being staged in her honor, and she found it pleasant and amusing." When Romero presents her with a bull's ear "cut by popular acclamation," she carries it off to her hotel, stuffs it far back in the drawer of the bed table, and forgets about it. The ear was taken, however, from the same bull which had killed one of the crowd a few days before, during the dangerous bull-run through the streets; later the entire town attended the man's funeral, along with drinking and dancing societies from nearby communities. For the crowd, the death of this bull was a communal triumph and his ear a token of communal strength; for Brett the ear is a private trophy. In effect, she has robbed the community of its triumph, as she will now rob it of its hero. As an *aficionado*, Barnes understands this threat too well. These are decadent times in the bull ring, marred by false esthetics; Romero alone has "the old thing," the old "purity of line through the maximum of exposure": his corruption by Brett will complete the decadence. But mainly the young fighter means something more personal to Barnes. In the bull ring he combines grace, control, and sincerity with manliness; in the fight with Cohn he proves his integrity where skill is lacking. His values are exactly those of the hunter in "Francis Macomber," or of the fisherman in *The Old Man and the Sea*. As one of these few remaining images of independent manhood, he offers Barnes the comfort of vicarious redemption. Brett seems to smash this as she leaves with Pedro for Madrid. To ward off depression, Barnes can only get drunk and retire to bed; the fiesta goes on outside, but it means nothing now: the "good place" has been ruined.

As Book III begins, Barnes tries to reclaim his dignity and to cleanse himself of the damage at Pamplona. He goes to San Sebastian and sits quietly there in a café, listening to band concerts; or he goes swimming there along, diving deep in the green waters. Then a telegram from Brett arrives, calling him to Madrid to help her out of trouble. At once he is like Cohn again, ready to serve his lady at the expense of self-respect. Yet in Madrid he learns to accept, emotionally, what he has always faintly understood. As he listens to Brett, he begins to drink heavily, as if her story has driven home a painful lesson. Brett herself feels "rather good" about sending Pedro away: she has at least been able to avoid being "one of these bitches that ruins children." This is a moral triumph for her, as Barnes agrees; but he can scarcely ignore its implications for himself. For when Brett refuses to let her hair grow long for Pedro, it means that her role in life is fixed: she can no longer reclaim her lost womanhood; she can no longer live with a fine man without destroying him. This seems to kill the illusion which is behind Jake's suffering throughout the novel: namely, that if he hadn't been wounded, if he had somehow survived the war with his manhood intact, then he and Brett would have become true lovers. The closing lines confirm his total disillusionment:

> "Oh, Jake," Brett said, "we could have had such a damned good time together."
> Ahead was a mounted policeman in khaki directing traffic. He raised his baton. The car slowed suddenly pressing Brett against me.
> "Yes," I said. "Isn't it pretty to think so?"

"Pretty" is a romantic word which means here "foolish to consider what could *never* have happened," and not "what can't happen now." The signal for this interpretation comes from the policeman who directs traffic between Brett's speech and Barnes's reply. With his khaki clothes and his preventive baton, he stands for the war and the society which made it, for the force which stops the lovers' car, and which robs them of their normal sexual roles. As Barnes now sees, love itself is dead for their generation. Even without his wound, he would still be unmanly, and Brett unable to let her hair grow long.

Yet, according to the opening epigraphs, if one generation is lost and another comes, the earth abides forever; and according to Hemingway himself, the abiding earth is the novel's hero. Perhaps he is wrong on this point, or at least misleading. There are no joyous hymns to the seasons in this novel, no celebrations of fertility and change. The scenic descriptions are accurate enough, but rather flat; there is no deep feeling in them, only fondness, for the author takes less delight in nature than in outdoor sports. He is more concerned, that is, with baiting hooks and catching trout than with the Irati River and more pleased with the grace and skill of the bullfighter than with the bull's magnificence. In fact, it is the bullfighter who seems to abide in the novel, for surely the bulls are dead like the trout before them, having fulfilled their roles as beloved opponents. But Romero is very much alive as the novel ends. When he leaves the hotel in Madrid, he "pays the bill" for his affair with Brett, which means that he has earned all its benefits. He also dominates the final conversation between the lovers, and so dominates the closing section. We learn here that his sexual initiation has been completed and his independence assured. From now on, he can work out his life alone, moving again and again through his passes in the ring, gaining strength, order, and purpose as he meets his own conditions. He provides no literal prescription to follow here, no call to bullfighting as the answer to Barnes's problems; but he does provide an image of integrity, against which Barnes and his generation are weighed and found wanting. In this sense, Pedro is the real hero of the parable, the final moral touchstone, the man whose code gives meaning to a world where love and religion are defunct, where the proofs of manhood are difficult and scarce, and where every man must learn to define his own moral conditions and then live up to them.

Philip Young

[*The Sun Also Rises:*
A Commentary]

The Sun Also Rises, which appeared in 1926, reintroduces us to the hero. In Hemingway's novels this man is a slightly less personal hero than Nick was, and his adventures are to be less closely identified with Hemingway's, for more events are changed, or even "made up." But he still projects qualities of the man who created him, many of his experiences are still either literal or transformed autobiography, and his wound is still the crucial fact about him. Even when, as Robert Jordan of *For Whom the Bell Tolls*, he is somewhat disguised, we have little or no trouble in recognizing him.

Recognition is immediate and unmistakable in *The Sun Also Rises*. Here the wound, again with its literal and symbolic meaning, is transferred from the spine to the genitals: Jake Barnes was emasculated in the war. But he is the same man, a grown Nick Adams, and again the actual injury functions as concrete evidence that the hero is a casualty. He is a writer living in Paris in the twenties as, for example, Harry was; he was, like Nick, transplanted from midwestern America to the Austro-Italian front; when things are at their worst for him, like Fraser he cries in the night. When he refuses the services of a prostitute, and she asks, "What's the

From *Ernest Hemingway* (New York: Holt, Rinehart and Winston, Inc., 1952) 54-60. Reprinted by permission of the author.

matter? You sick?" he is not thinking of his impotence alone when he answers, "Yes." He is the insomniac as before, and for the same reasons: "I blew out the lamp. Perhaps I would be able to sleep. My head started to work. The old grievance." And later he remembers that time, which we witnessed, when "for six months I never slept with the light off." He is the man who is troubled in the night, who leaves Brett alone in his sitting room and lies face down on the bed, having "a bad time."

In addition, Jake like Nick is the protagonist who has broken with society and with the usual middle-class ways; and, again, he has made the break in connection with his wounding. He has very little use for most people. At times he has little use even for his friends; at times he has little use for himself. He exists on a fringe of the society he has renounced; as a newspaper reporter he works just enough to make enough money to eat and drink well on, and spends the rest of his time in cafés, or fishing, or watching bullfights. Though it is not highly developed yet, he and those few he respects have a code, too. Jake complains very little, although he suffers a good deal; there are certain things that are "done" and many that are "not done." Lady Brett Ashley also knows the code, and distinguishes people according to it; a person is "one of us," as she puts it, or is not—and most are not. The whole trouble with Robert Cohn, the boxing, maladroit Jew of the novel, is that he is not. He points up the code most clearly by so lacking it: he will not go away when Brett is done with him; he is "messy" in every way. After he has severely beaten up Romero, the small young bullfighter, and Romero will not give in, Cohn cries, wretchedly proclaims his love for Brett in public, and tries to shake Romero's hand. He gets that hand in the face, an act which is approved as appropriate comment on his behavior.

Cohn does not like Romero because Brett does. She finally goes off with the bullfighter, and it is when she leaves him too that she makes a particularly clear statement of what she and the other "right" people have salvaged from the wreck of their compromised lives. She has decided that she is ruining Romero's career, and besides she is too old for him. She walks out, and says to Jake:

> "It makes one feel rather good deciding not to be a bitch. . . . It's sort of what we have instead of God."

In early editions, *The Sun Also Rises* had on its title page, in addition to the passage on futility in *Ecclesiastes* from which the title is taken, Gertrude Stein's famous "You are all a lost generation." The novel provides an explanation for this observation, in addition to illustrating it in action. As in the story called "In Another Country," the picture of the hero wounded and embittered by his experience of violence is broadened to include other people. Brett Ashley, for example, and her fiancé Mike Campbell are both casualties from ordeals similar to those which damaged Jake. Brett has behind her the very unpleasant death of her first fiancé; Mike's whole character was shattered by the war. *A Farewell to Arms* can be read as background to the earlier novel: some of Brett's past is filled in by Catherine Barkley, whose fiancé had been blown to bits in the war, and most of Jake's by Frederic Henry.

The fact that characters in *The Sun Also Rises* are recognizable people, taken from "real life," does not contradict the fact that they are in this pattern. Various personages known to Paris of the twenties have thought that they recognized without difficulty the originals—Donald Ogden Stewart, Harold Stearns, Harold Loeb, Lady Duff-Twisden, Ford Madox Ford, and Pat Guthrie—and even Jake had his counterpart in actuality. But Hemingway, like most authors, has changed the characters to suit his purposes, and it is clear that whatever his origins, Jake, for instance, owes most to the man who created him, and is the hero.

He is the hero emasculated, however, and this must primarily account for the fact that he does not always seem entirely real. As he feels befits his status, he is largely a passive arranger of things for others, who only wants to "play it along and just not make trouble for people." But as narrator, at least, he is convincing, and if there is something blurred about him it helps to bring the participants into a focus that is all the sharper. Hemingway has always been good with secondary characters, finding them in a bright flash that reveals all we need know. Here, as he somehow manages to make similar people easily distinguishable, the revelations are brilliant. One remembers Brett and Cohn longest, for they get the fullest development, but Count Mippipopolous is wonderful, and wonderful too—save for their anti-Semitism, largely missing from the twenty-five cent edition, which advertises that "Not one word has been changed or omitted"—are Mike and Bill.

Chiefly it is Hemingway's ear, a trap that catches every mannerism of speech, that is responsible for the fact that these wastrels come so alive and distinct. That famous ear also caught a great many "swells" and "grands" that have dated—for slang is one thing almost certain to go bad with the passage of time—and some of the dialogue of camaraderie ("Old Bill!" "You bum!") is also embarrassing. But taken as a whole the talk is superb and, as a whole, so is the rest of the writing in the book. Hemingway's wide-awake senses fully evoke an American's Paris, a vacationer's Spain. Jake moves through these places with the awareness of a professional soldier reconnoitering new terrain. The action is always foremost, but it is supported by real country and real city. The conversational style, which gives us the illusion that Jake is just telling us the story of what he has been doing lately, gracefully hides the fact that the pace is carefully calculated and swift, the sentences and scenes hard and clean. This is true of the over-all structure, too: the book is informal and relaxed only on the surface, and beneath it lies a scrupulous and satisfying orchestration. It is not until nearly the end, for example, when Cohn becomes the center of what there is of action, that opening with him seems anything but a simply random way of getting started. This discussion of Cohn has eased us into Jake's life in Paris, and especially his situation with Brett. Suddenly the lines are all drawn. An interlude of trout fishing moves us smoothly into Spain and the bullfights. At Pamplona the tension which all try to ignore builds up, slowly, and breaks finally as the events come to their climax simultaneously with the fiesta's. Then, in an intensely muted coda, a solitary Jake, rehabilitating himself, washes away his hangovers in the ocean. Soon it is all gone, he is returned to Brett as before, and we discover that we have come full circle, like all the rivers, the winds, and the sun, to the place where we began.

This is motion which goes no place. Constant activity has brought us along with such pleasant, gentle insistence that not until the end do we realize that we have not been taken in, exactly, but taken nowhere; and that, finally, is the point. This is structure as meaning, organization as content. And, as the enormous effect the book had on its generation proved, such a meaning or content was important to 1926. The book touched with delicate acuracy on something big, on things other people were feeling, but too dimly for articulation. Hemingway had deeply felt and understood what was in the wind. Like Brett, who was the kind of woman who sets styles, the book itself was profoundly creative, and had the kind of power that is prototypal.

But for another generation, looking backward, this quality of the novel is largely gone out of it. The pessimism is based chiefly on the story of a hopeless love, and for Jake this is basis enough. But his situation with Brett sometimes seems forced—brought up periodically for air that it may be kept alive—as if Hemingway, who must have been through most of Jake's important experiences, but not exactly this one, had to keep reminding himself that it existed. And worse: though the rest of the pessimism rises eloquently out of the novel's structure, it does not seem to rise out of the day-to-day action at all. There is a gaping cleavage here between manner and message, between joy in life and a pronouncement of life's futility. Jake's disability excepted, always, the book now seems really the long *Fiesta* it was called in the English edition, and one's net impression today is of all the fun there is to be had in getting good and lost.

And yet *The Sun Also Rises* is still Hemingway's *Waste Land*, and Jake is Hemingway's Fisher King. This may be just coincidence, though the novelist had read the poem, but once again here is the protagonist gone impotent, and his land gone sterile. Eliot's London is Hemingway's Paris, where spiritual life in general, and Jake's sexual life in particular, are alike impoverished. Prayer breaks down and fails, a knowledge of traditional distinctions between good and evil is largely lost, copulation is morally neutral and, cut off from the past chiefly by the spiritual disaster of the war, life has become mostly meaningless. "What shall we do?" is the same constant question, to which the answer must be, again, "Nothing." To hide it, instead of playing chess one drinks, mechanically and always. Love is a possibility only for the two who cannot love; once again homosexuality intensifies this atmosphere of sterility; once more the Fisher King is also a man who fishes. And again the author plays with quotations from the great of the past, as when in reply to Jake's remark that he is a taxidermist Bill objects, "That was in another country. And besides all the animals were dead."

To be sure, the liquor is good, and so are the food and the conversation. But in one way Hemingway's book is even more desperate than Eliot's. The lesson of an "asceticism" to control the aimless expression of lust would be to Jake Barnes only one more bad joke, and the fragments he has shored against his ruins are few, and quite inadequate. In the poem a message of salvation comes out of the life-giving rain which falls on western civilization. In Hemingway's waste land there is fun, but there is no hope. No rain falls on Europe this time, and when it does fall, in *A Farewell to Arms*, it brings not life but death.

Malcolm Cowley

Commencing with the Simplest Things

At the end of December, 1921, when Hemingway was twenty-two years old and newly married, he came to Paris for a second visit. The first, in May, 1918, had lasted only until he picked up a Red Cross ambulance, which he drove in convoy to the Italian front. There he had been gravely wounded early in July, and he had spent three months in and out of military hospitals. After his return to Chicago he had written many stories and poems and had even started a novel, but he had so far published nothing over his own name except in high-school papers and in the weekly magazine of the Toronto *Star*. He now planned to finish out his apprenticeship as a writer, and the second visit—interrupted by four unhappy months in Toronto—would last for nearly seven years. His apprenticeship, however, would end spectacularly in 1926, with the publication of *The Sun Also Rises*.

In these days when many things have ended, it is a melancholy pleasure to go back over the records of that era when everything

91

was starting, for Hemingway and others, and when almost anything seemed possible. He came to Paris with letters of introduction from Sherwood Anderson, whom he had known well in Chicago,
and also with a roving commission from the Toronto *Star* to write
color stories, for which he would be paid at space rates if the stories
were printed. In those days such commissions were easy to obtain,
since they did not obligate a newspaper to spend money, and usually they led to nothing but a few rejected or grudgingly printed
manuscripts. Hemingway's stories were good enough to feature,
and they quickly led to definite assignments, with travel expenses.

Suddenly elevated to the position of staff reporter and author-
ized to send cables—but not too many of them—Hemingway was
dispatched to the Genoa Economic Conference in March, 1922, to
the Near East in September, for the last days of the Greco-Turkish
War, and to Lausanne at the end of November, for the peace conference that followed. He also worked for Hearst's International
News Service on the last two of those assignments, earning while he
learned. In Asia Minor he studied the Greek retreat as if it were a
laboratory experiment in warfare. At Lausanne he studied the
mechanics of international relations, with the help of barside lec-
tures from William Bolitho, already famous as a correspondent. In
both places he studied the curious language known as cabelese,
in which every word has to do the work of six or seven. At three
dollars a word he would put a message something like this on the
wires: KEMAL INSWARDS UNBURNED SMYRNA GUILTY
GREEKS. The translation appearing in the Hearst papers would
be: "Mustapha Kemal in an exclusive interview today with the
correspondent of the International News Service [KEMAL IN-
SWARDS] denied vehemently that the Turkish forces had any
part in the burning of Smyrna [UNBURNED SMYRNA]. The
city, Kemal stated, was fired by incendiaries in the troops of the
Greek rear guard before the first Turkish patrols entered the city
[GUILTY GREEKS]."

Cabelese was an exercise in omitting everything that can be
taken for granted. It contributed to Hemingway's literary method,
just as the newspaper assignments contributed to his subject matter. Going back over the records, one is astonished to find how
much he learned during that first year abroad. He said afterwards
that "A great enough writer seems to be born with knowledge.
But he really is not; he has only been born with the ability to learn
in a quicker ratio to the passage of time than other men and without conscious application, and with an intelligence to accept or

reject what is already presented as knowledge." Hemingway had that gift to such an extent that I sometimes think of him as an instinctive student who never went to college. His motto through life was not that of Sherwood Anderson's groping adolescents, "I want to know why," but rather, "I want to know *how*"—how to write, first of all, but also how to fish, how to box, how to ski, how to act in the bull ring, how to remember his own sensations, how to nurse his talent, how to live while learning to write, and more broadly how to *live*, in the sense of mastering the rules that must be followed by anyone who wants to respect himself. Many of his stories can be read and have been read by thousands as, essentially, object lessons in practical ethics and professional decorum.

There is much more to be said about Hemingway as a lifelong student. Charles A. Fenton wrote a useful book on the subject, *The Apprenticeship of Ernest Hemingway*, but it deals only with his early training as a writer and omits his other fields of study. Besides those already mentioned, the fields would eventually include wing shooting, big-game fishing and hunting, food, wines and liquors, Italian, French, Spanish, Basque, Swahili, military geography, navigation, ballistics, and death as a natural phenomenon. He had a true student's humility, but also a student's pride and a burning wish to excel. If he did not stand high in a field of study, or did not need it in his daily life, he quickly abandoned it, as he abandoned the cello, football, bridge, tennis (except for exercise), and amateur bullfighting, for which, as he told the Old Lady of *Death in the Afternoon,* "I was too old, too heavy and too awkward." In other fields he went on to take postgraduate work —for example in bullfighting as a spectator sport—and became an acknowledged master.

Since there were no textbooks in many of his fields, or none that could be trusted, he went straight to the best teachers. Among those under whom he studied during his first Paris year were Gertrude Stein and Ezra Pound, both friends of Hemingway but not of each other, and a cross-eyed Negro jockey from Cincinnati named Jim Winkfield.

How much he learned from his two older literary friends is the subject of a long-standing argument, but I think he learned a great deal. He listened attentively, and he had too much confidence in himself to fear, as many young writers do, that he would end as somebody's disciple. He could afford to take from others because he gave so much in return. What he gave to Miss Stein is partly revealed in his letters to her, now in the Yale Library: he

helped to get her work published in the *transatlantic review* when
he was helping to edit it, and having learned that she had only a
bound manuscript of *The Making of Americans,* he typed long
sections of it for the printer. One thing he took from her was an
apparently colloquial American style, full of repeated words,
prepositional phrases, and present participles, the style in which
he wrote his early published stories. One thing he took from Pound
—in return for trying vainly to teach him how to box—was
the doctrine of the accurate image, which he applied in the
"chapters" printed between the stories that went into *In Our Time;*
but Hemingway also learned from him to blue-pencil most of his
adjectives and adverbs. What he learned from Jim Winkfield was
much simpler: it was the name of a winning horse.

I heard the story from the late Evan Shipman, poet, trotting-
horse columnist, and one of Hemingway's lifelong friends. Winkfield, he told me, had won the Kentucky Derby in 1901, on His
Eminence, and again the following year, on Alan-a-Dale. By 1922
Negro jockeys were not being employed on American tracks, and
Winkfield was in France training horses for Pierre Wertheimer,
who had a famous stable. There is no outside audience when colts
are trained in France, and there are no professional clockers at
their time trials; every stable has its own secrets. At Wertheimer's
stable the secret was Epinard, a sensationally promising colt with
an unfashionable sire. Winkfield, who was seeing a lot of Hemingway, told him that Epinard was going to run his first race at
Deauville that summer. Having borrowed all the money he could,
Hemingway laid it on Epinard's nose.

That wasn't his only big day at the track. In June of the same
year—writing from Milan, where he said that most of the races
were fixed—he reported to Gertrude Stein that he had picked
seventeen winners out of twenty-one starts. Most of his winnings
went into the bank, for he already planned to stop working for
newspapers. Miss Stein had something to do with the decision.
"If you keep on doing newspaper work," she told him, "you will
never see things, you will only see words, and that will not do—
that is, of course, if you intend to be a writer."

Hemingway had never intended to be anything else, but writing
every day was a luxury he still couldn't afford. The *Star,* impressed
by a series of articles he had lately submitted on the French occupation of the Ruhr, offered him a job in the home office at a top
reporter's salary, for those days, of $125 a week. In September,
1923, he left for Toronto with the intention of working two years

and saving enough money to finish a novel. Soon he came into conflict with Harry C. Hindmarsh, then assistant managing editor of the *Star*, who tried to break his spirit with what seems to have been a series of nagging persecutions. Hemingway resigned explosively at the end of December, and the following month he was back in Paris, resolved to starve if he must but write for himself.

II

Those were the days when young American writers regarded Paris as a necessary stage in their educations and the only place in the world where they could meet others who were doing serious work. They came to Paris by scores and later by hundreds, crowding the boat trains and pouring through the Gare Saint-Lazare like stampeding Herefords. They took rooms in disreputable hotels on the Left Bank, then hurried off to the Café du Dôme, where they remained for most of the night and other nights as well. After months or a year they usually decided that Paris wasn't the best place for working after all, and they grandly moved south to the Riviera, Majorca, Capri, or wherever they could write a book without interruptions. But they came back with the book half started, and especially in the long June evenings one could see them outside the Dôme, in noisy groups at the tables covered with saucers, or sitting alone and recognizable not only by their simple bulk, as compared with the French, but also by the uneasy glance with which they searched for an acquaintance willing to read an unfinished manuscript or lend them fifty francs to carry them over until the next check came from home.

Some of the young writers were already known and were soon to become famous: in Paris at the time were E. E. Cummings, John Dos Passos, John Peale Bishop, Kay Boyle, Scott Fitzgerald, Glenway Wescott, Louis Bromfield, Robert M. Coates, and Archibald MacLeish, to mention only a few. Hemingway knew all of these and was a close friend of three or four, but it was a younger group that specially looked up to him. The group was composed of writers then in the process of being "discovered," which is to say that they were getting their first stories or poems printed in little magazines that bloomed and disappeared like wildflowers; at least a brace of new talents was discovered in every issue of every new magazine. Running over a list of names some years ago, I found that many of the group had gone into business or teaching, that others were dead, like Shipman and John Herrmann—not even bullfighters have a higher mortality rate than unread writers—and that still others, then including Morley Callaghan, were writing well but in comparative obscurity while waiting to be discovered again.

You couldn't say that Hemingway was a leader among them, because he didn't belong to the group, but they were proud to be seen with him. He seldom appeared at the Dôme except in the early morning for coffee. It was an event of the evening when he passed the café, tall, broad, and handsome, usually wearing a patched jacket and sneakers, and often walking on the balls of his feet like a boxer. Arms waved in greeting from the sidewalk tables, and friends ran out to urge him to sit down with them. "The occasions were charming little scenes, as if spontaneous even though repeated," says Nathan Asch, who remembers those days. "In view of the whole terrace, Hemingway would be striding toward the Montparnasse railroad station, his mind seemingly busy with the mechanics of someone's arrival or departure, and he wouldn't quite recognize whoever greeted him. Then suddenly his beautiful smile appeared that made those watching him also smile; and with a will and an eagerness he put out his hands and warmly greeted his acquaintance, who, overcome by this reception, simply glowed; and who returned with Hem to the table as if with an overwhelming prize."

"No, I have no criticism to make of Hem's conduct," said another veteran of the Paris years. "I do think it's a crazy situation, though, that the elimination was so brutal, that of all the writers in Paris then, Hem is holding the world by the handle and everybody else is either obscure or dead. But you can't blame it on Hem."

What distinguished him from the young writers at the sidewalk tables, now obscure or dead, was of course his greater talent, but it was also his studious habit of mind and his willingness to work harder than any of the others. "He was gay, he was sentimental," Lincoln Steffens said of him, "but he was always at work." Once when they were dining at a Chinese restaurant in Paris, he insisted to Mrs. Steffens that anyone could write. "You can," he told her, feinting as if to give her a left to the jaw, for he was always shadow-boxing in those days. "It's hell. It takes it all out of you; it nearly kills you; but you can do it. Anybody can. Even you can, Stef. . . . I haven't done it yet, but I will." He seemed to think, Steffens reported, "that writing was a matter of honesty and labor, and maybe it is, utter honesty and hard labor."

Hemingway had met Steffens at the Lausanne Conference and had shown him some of his dispatches from the Near East. Steffens wanted to see more of his work, and Hemingway asked his wife, Hadley, to send it on from Paris. That was just before Christmas, 1922. Hadley packed his manuscripts in a suitcase and carried it herself, because she was afraid they would be lost if she sent them by express. At the Gare de Lyon in Paris, she left the compartment for a moment to get a drink of water, and the suitcase was stolen. It contained everything he had written and saved until that time —an unfinished novel, eighteen stories, thirty poems—and it was never recovered. There was a little salvage. *Poetry* had accepted six poems, the *Cosmopolitan* had rejected a story, "My Old Man," which was then in the mail, and lying on his desk was another story, "Up in Michigan." For the rest, all the early work that he valued was irretrievably lost.

It was a disaster for Hemingway, but in some ways a fortunate one. With his early work destroyed as if by fire, he could start from the beginning and build another structure on new lines. "I was trying to learn to write," he says on the second page of *Death in the Afternoon,* in a passage referring to those months, "commencing with the simplest things." That last phrase is almost unique in its mixture of humility and hard-headedness. I have known many apprentice writers, but not one other who was willing, at twenty-three, to put aside everything he had learned or accomplished and start again with the simplest things.

Hemingway studied writing in Paris as if he were studying geometry without a textbook and inventing theorems as he went along. He accepted as a postulate that the function of any literary work is to evoke some particular emotion from the reader; but how could that best be done? Most writers were content to describe an emotion as it was felt by themselves or their heroes, in hopes that the reader would be moved by it, but this was a method that made him the mere auditor of someone else's fear or longing or rage. Hemingway wanted to make his readers feel the emotion directly—not as if they were being told about an event, but as if they were taking part in it. The best way to produce this effect, he decided as a first theorem, was to set down exactly, in their proper sequence, the sights, sounds, touches, tastes, and smells that had produced an emotion he remembered feeling. Then, without auctorial comments and without ever saying that he or his hero had been frightened, sad, or angry, he could make the reader feel the emotion for himself.

"I was trying to write then," he says in that same passage of *Death in the Afternoon,* "and I found the greatest difficulty, aside from knowing truly what you really felt, rather than what you were supposed to feel, and had been taught to feel, was to put down what really happened in action; what the actual things were which produced the emotion that you experienced. In writing for a news-paper you told what happened and, with one trick and another, you communicated the emotion aided by the element of timeliness which gives a certain emotion to any account of something that has happened on that day; but the real thing, the sequence of motion and fact which made the emotion and which would be as valid in a year or in ten years or, with luck and if you stated it purely enough, always, was beyond me and I was working very hard to try to get it."

That often quoted passage suggests a whole system of practical aesthetics—not the loftiest one, not one to which Hemingway would always confine himself, but a sound system within its self-imposed limitations and an excellent guide for any young writer. Hemingway is suggesting, in substance, that a piece of writing might be regarded as a machine for producing a particular effect, and that its capacity for producing the effect should be permanent. "When you describe something that has happened that day," he would say elsewhere, "the timeliness makes people see it in their own imaginations. A month later that element of time is gone and your account would be flat and they would not see in their minds nor remember it." Good writing, as Ezra Pound was already saying, is "news that *stays* news." It can stay news if it has achieved certain definite qualities, that is, if it is absolutely honest —a virtue that depends on "knowing truly what you really felt, rather than what you were supposed to feel, and had been taught to feel"—and if it presents "the real thing, the sequence of motion and fact which made the emotion." But a writer's luck, or uncon-scious, also plays a part in the process, and the real thing had to be stated "purely enough" if it is to remain valid through the years.

"Purely enough," for Hemingway, meant without tricks of any sort, without conventionally emotive language, and with a bare minimum of adjectives and adverbs. It also meant that the per-manent work had to be written like cabelese, with everything omitted that the reader could take for granted, and with each detail so carefully selected that it did the work of six or seven. One of Hemingway's early studies was the art of omission. "If a writer of prose knows enough about what he is writing about," he says in another chapter of *Death in the Afternoon*, "he may omit things that he knows and the reader, if the writer is writing truly enough, will have a feeling of those things as strongly as though the writer had stated them. The dignity of movement of an ice-berg is due to only one-eight of it being above water."

That sort of dignity is difficult to attain, and Hemingway "was working very hard to try to get it." With his talent for methodology, for the *how*, he thought it could best be achieved, at the beginning, in very short pieces. The first ones he wrote after starting again with the simplest things were the vignettes, or "chapters," that would later be printed in italics between the stories in the first of his books to be issued by a New York publisher, *In Our Time*. Much earlier six of the "chapters," all those he had finished at the moment, appeared in the April, 1923, issue of the *Little Review*. One of these was the paragraph that afterwards became "Chapter II," the one beginning "Minarets stuck up in the rain out of Adrianople across the mud flats." Perhaps it was the very first work in his new manner, and it exists in three separate versions, with a complicated history of changes that Charles A. Fenton has studied at length.

The earliest version consists of the first three paragraphs of a story that Hemingway cabled to the *Star* from Adrianople on October 20, 1922. It was not written in cabelese, as it would have been if he were sending it to the International News Service, and it was a masterly piece of reporting. Lincoln Steffens, who read it at Lausanne in December, recollected much of it ten years later when writing the last chapters of his *Autobiography*. The paragraphs, however, were not in Hemingway's new manner. In their total length of 241 words there were no less than thirty adjectives, and some of these were compound words like "never-ending" and "muddy-flanked." There were also signposts to guide the reader toward having the proper emotions, that is, there were charged words and phrases like "ghastly," "in horror," and "to keep off the driving rain." These "tricks," as Hemingway called them, were permissible and even necessary in a newspaper story designed to produce its effect at a single hasty glance.

In the second version, the one that Hemingway published in the *Little Review*, all the guideposts to emotion have disappeared and so have most of the adjectives. Some of the descriptive details have also been omitted, in order to bring the others into sharper focus. The process of sharpening and tightening the prose while suppressing even the implied comments of the author continued for a long time, and the results of it appear in the third and almost final version. This is the one included in a very short booklet published in France in 1924 and bearing the same title as Hemingway's first book-length collection of stories: *in our time*, but in this case without capital letters. The version reads:

> Minarets stuck up in the rain out of Adrianople across the mud flats. The carts were jammed for thirty miles along the Karagatch road. Water buffalo and cattle were hauling the carts through the mud. No end and no beginning. Just carts loaded with everything they owned. The old men and women, soaked through, walked along keeping the cattle moving. The Maritza was running yellow almost up to the bridge. Carts were jammed solid on the bridge with camels bobbing along through them. Greek cavalry herded along the procession. Women and kids were in the carts crouched with mattresses, mirrors, sewing machines, bundles. There was a woman having a kid with a young girl holding a blanket over her and crying. Scared sick looking at it. It rained all through the evacuation.

Here the "chapter," as it is now called, has been shortened to 131 words, or only half the length of the newspaper version. There are only ten descriptive adjectives instead of thirty, and every one of them is simple and definite. Four of the adjectives—"loaded," "soaked," "crouched," and "scared"—are past participles and have somewhat the effect of verbs in the passive voice: the right effect, since the refugees are the passive subjects of action. There are also ten present participles, three of which occur in the same sentence: "... *having* a kid with a young girl *holding* a blanket over her and *crying*." They give a sense of action that continues under our eyes. This use, and sometimes abuse, of present participles was one of the habits that Hemingway had probably acquired from Gertrude Stein, along with a fondness for prepositional phrases used in series ("*in* the rain *out of* Adrianople *across* the mud flats") and a distrust of relative clauses. All the sentences are short, averaging only ten words. (Incidentally this is not a characteristic of Hemingway's later prose, in which there are sentences almost as long as Faulkner's.) Three sentences have been stripped of their verbs, and the others without exception are simple and declarative.

There were further changes, if slight ones, in 1925 when the Adrianople "chapter" was included in the much longer American *In Our Time* (with the capitalized title), and again in 1930 when the book was reissued by Scribner's. Did the changes work, taken as a whole? To expand the question, what effects did Hemingway produce on his readers as a result of his patient revisions in this and the other brief "chapters," sixteen in all, that were written during the six months after he lost his manuscripts? I think the effects on sympathetic and attentive readers, at first a minority, were close to those he had planned to produce. Other readers blamed Hemingway, insensitively, for being tough and insensitive. But the attentive ones were moved, though they seldom knew why, and they felt they were seeing events for themselves instead of just hearing about them. They felt that the exaggeratedly simple and awkward-looking style made everything seem authentic; and they also felt that the "chapters" had an impact that was not in proportion to their size, as if part of it depended on words that went unspoken. Written without tricks—except the great ones of understatement and omission—those very brief works proved to be news that stayed news. They have exerted a permanent influence even on writers who turned aginst Hemingway, and they brought about something like a revolution in American prose fiction.

Hemingway himself wrote no more "chapters" after his return from Toronto in 1924. Instead he went on to the second stage in his program, which consisted in writing stories. He began by applying the methods developed in his vignettes, but this time, instead of merely presenting a scene, he included some of the events leading up to it, in strict chronological sequence. He also included dialogue, for which he had an instinctively fine ear. But simple chronology, or narrative sequence, was the principal element that distinguished the stories from the "chapters," and Hemingway displayed an extraordinary gift for putting first things first, second things second, and for stopping short of what other writers would regard as the climax in order to let the reader go on for himself. That explains the power of suggestion of early stories like "Cat in the Rain"; the climax is on the next page after the end.

In discussing the purely technical aspects of Hemingway's early work, I have omitted what he calls the element of luck. He had that too, in the shape of an unusually rich unconscious and a stock of subject matter, both giving him an advantage over two of his teachers. Ezra Pound had only two closely related subjects at the time, art and the life of art. Gertrude Stein's principal subject was herself. Hemingway's subject was also himself, or his inner world, but that self had a passion for acquiring knowledge and for rushing forward to meet external challenges, so that his inner world already included a broad and highly colored segment of the outer world. He was a very complicated young man at twenty-six, with something close to a genius for simplification. Many readers felt that his stories were completely new in American fiction. Shortly after *In Our Time* appeared in New York, Alfred Harcourt, an astute publisher who would have liked to have issued the book, said in a letter to Louis Bromfield, "Hemingway's first novel might rock the country." The letter was sent to Paris in the late autumn of 1925, at a time when Hemingway had reached a third stage in his career. Having learned how to write stories, he was then revising a hastily written draft of *The Sun Also Rises*.

III

I don't mean to suggest that Hemingway was spending all of his time at his desk. He boxed regularly at a Paris gymnasium. He played a good deal of tennis with, among others, Ezra Pound, Bill Bullitt, and Harold Loeb, the former publisher of *Broom*, who had been a middle-weight wrestler at Princeton. By this time Hemingway had acquired a wide circle of friends, or rather a number of nonintersecting circles composed respectively of tennis friends, boxing friends, racetrack friends, newspaper friends, and older and younger writing friends. Some of the younger ones he published in the two issues of the *transatlantic review* that he edited while Ford Madox Ford, its founder and publisher, was in New York. Some other friends joined with him one summer to rent a trout stream in the Black Forest. He spent several winters skiing at a little town called Schruns, in the Vorarlberg, where he was once offered the job of skiing instructor.

One is again surprised to find how much he learned in those years and how quickly he reached a professional level in most of his fields of study. At one time he was a prizefight manager, with a little stable of boxers that included Larry Gaines, a Negro heavyweight from Toronto who later beat Max Schmeling in one of Schmeling's early fights. That business career ended on a famous evening when Hemingway jumped into the ring to save a young boxer from being killed in a fixed fight, and, with a water bottle, knocked out Francis Charles, the middleweight champion of France. After that he abandoned French boxing as a crooked sport and devoted more and more attention to the bullfights in Spain.

I can't find a record of the first bullfight he saw, but in 1923 he was in Pamplona for the *feria* of San Fermin, which lasted always from July 6 to July 12. In 1924 he was back with Donald Ogden Stewart, already a successful humorist, and both men took part in the amateur bullfights that were held each morning. Hemingway returned to Paris very excited, with photographs of the big pepper-and-salt bull that had carried him across the arena on its horns, after breaking Stewart's ribs. In 1925 he was back in Pamplona for another fiesta and another adventure with the bulls; but first he had made a trout-fishing expedition to the Irati River with his wife and Don Stewart and Bill Smith, a friend he had known since his Michigan days. Construction work on a dam had ruined the fishing and they didn't catch a trout.

The fiesta was in some ways even less successful. The group in Pamplona, besides the fishermen, included Harold Loeb, Patrick Guthrie, who was an English remittance man, and his friend Lady Duff Twysden, who was believed to be the heroine of Michael Arlen's immensely popular novel, *The Girl in the Green Hat*. Usually she did wear a floppy-brimmed green felt hat, but she was more widely known for her love affairs and her capacity for holding liquor. Everybody drank a great deal at the fiesta and almost everybody quarreled. "Some fiesta," said Harold Loeb, who later described it in his memoirs. Things went better at the bull ring, where the principal attraction was Nino de la Palma, then in his first season as a matador. Awarded the ear of the last bull he killed, to great applause, he presented it to Hadley Hemingway, who wrapped it in a handkerchief and took it back to the hotel.

Hemingway and his wife went on to Madrid and then to Valencia. There on July 21, which was his twenty-sixth birthday, he started to write *The Sun Also Rises*, exactly nine days after some of the events that would be described (and considerably revised) in the novel. One of his early theorems was that the background of an experience should be presented truly, "the way it was," but that the story should be "made up," so as to become truer than what actually happened. Work on the novel continued uninterruptedly in Madrid, San Sebastian, Hendaye, and Paris, where the first draft was finished on September 6, after forty-eight working days. "I knew nothing about writing a novel when I started it," Hemingway said many years later, "and so wrote too fast and each day to the point of complete exhaustion. So the first draft was very bad. I wrote it in six weeks and I had to rewrite it completely. But in the rewriting I learned much."

Before setting to work on the revision, he put the manuscript aside for nearly three months to season. It was during this interval that he wrote a book-length satire, *The Torrents of Spring*, in a little more than a week. He went back to the novel in December, while he was skiing at Schruns, and worked hard on it during the next two months. In February, 1926, he made a hasty trip to

New York, had an interview with Maxwell Perkins of Scribner's, and signed a contract for both the satire (to be published first) and the novel. Work on the latter continued during March and included a great deal of ruthless cutting, which amounted in the end to forty thousand words. Most of them were deleted from the first or Paris section of the manuscript. A final draft, consisting of eighty thousand words, went to the typist on April 1 and was published on October 22. *The Sun Also Rises* did not rock the country, but it received a number of hat-in-air reviews, and it soon became a handbook of conduct for the new generation. That winter an observer in Greenwich Village noted that many of the younger writers had already begun to talk, walk, and shadow-box like Hemingway, when they weren't flourishing capes in front of an imaginary bull.

I have read the book so often, for pleasure and professionally, that it is hard for me now to make fresh observations about it. One thing I notice more clearly than before is its technique, which once again reveals Hemingway's systematic or studentlike cast of mind and his habit of always starting with the simple before moving to the complex. In writing this first novel he applied the principles developed in his vignettes, along with others developed in his stories. Once again, as he went on to another stage, his work incorporated a new element besides its greater length. Whereas each of his stories had dealt with one or two persons, or three at the most, his novel deals with the rather complicated relations among a *group* of persons. That might even lead to a general description of the novel—any novel—as a literary form: it is a long but unified narrative, designed to be read at more than one sitting, which presents a situation affecting a group of characters and leading to a change in their relations.

The situation in the background of *The Sun Also Rises* is the Great War, in which most of the characters have served and in which some of them have been physically or morally wounded. All the characters except the matador, Pedro Romero, have lost their original code of values. Feeling the loss, they are now trying to live by a simpler code—essentially that of soldiers on furlough— and it is this effort which unites them as a group. "I told you he was one of us," Lady Brett says of Count Mippipopolous after he has unashamedly stripped off his shirt and shown them where an arrow had passed completely through his body. The unashamedness, the wound, and the courage it suggests are all things they have in common. The war in which they served has deadened some of their feelings, has left them capable of enjoying only the simplest and strongest pleasures, and has also given them an attitude of resigned acceptance toward all sorts of disasters, including those caused by their own follies. Robert Cohn, however, has never been wounded and has never learned to be resigned; therefore he refuses to let Brett go, fights with his rivals for her, including Romero, and is cast out of the group. Romero is their simple-minded saint. Brett is almost on the point of permanently corrupting him, but she obeys another article of the code and draws back. "You know, it makes one feel rather good deciding not to be a bitch," she says. "It's sort of what we have instead of God."

The Sun Also Rises is not, as I have heard it called, Hemingway's best novel. After all it is his first, and there are signs in it of his struggle to master a new medium. In spite of the forty thousand words deleted from the manuscript, there are still some details that do not seem essential, as notably in the street-by-street accounts of Jake Barnes's wanderings through Paris. There are also a few obvious guideposts for the reader, as when Jake says of Robert Cohn that "he was not so simple" after coming back from New York, "and he was not so nice." Although Cohn's fight with Romero is the physical climax of the action, it is reported at second hand—by Mike Campbell, who has heard the story from Brett, who was the only witness of the fight—instead of being presented before our eyes. More serious than these technical flaws, there is the sort of timeliness that is always in danger of going stale. Brett was a pathetic brave figure for her time. but the pathos has been cheapened by thousands of imitation Bretts in life and fiction. Bill Gorton's remarks are not so bright now as they once seemed. "You're an expatriate," he tells Jake ironically. "You've lost touch with the soil. You get precious. Fake European standards have ruined you. . . . You hang around cafés." In 1926 one felt that he was making exactly the right rejoinder to dozens of newspaper editorials then fresh in the public mind; in the 1960's these have been forgotten.

Not everything changes. After one has mentioned these wrinkles and scars revealed by age, how much of the novel seems as marvelously fresh as when it first appeared! Count Mippipopolous, his wound, and his champagne; the old couple from Montana on their first trip abroad; the busload of Basque peasants; the whole beautiful episode of the fishing trip in the mountains, in the harsh sunlight, and then by contrast the dark streets of Pamplona crowded with *riau-riau* dancers, who formed a circle round Brett as if she were a revered witch—as indeed she was, and as Jake in a way was the wounded Fisher King ruling over a sterile land —in all this there is nothing that has gone bad and not a word to be changed after so many years. It is all carved in stone, bigger and truer than life, and it is the work of a man who, having ended his busy term of apprenticeship, was already a master at twenty-six.